Understanding
Green Card
Marriage Fraud

Understanding Green Card Marriage Fraud

Malgorzata Zuber

LEXINGTON BOOKS
Lanham • Boulder • New York • London

Published by Lexington Books
An imprint of The Rowman & Littlefield Publishing Group, Inc.
4501 Forbes Boulevard, Suite 200, Lanham, Maryland 20706
www.rowman.com

6 Tinworth Street, London SE11 5AL, United Kingdom

ISBN 9781793626370 (cloth)
ISBN 9781793626394 (pbk)

British Library Cataloguing in Publication Information Available

Library of Congress Cataloging-in-Publication Data

Library of Congress Control Number: 2020952126

Contents

Contents

Preface

Historically, U.S. immigration policies were liberal prior to the 1880s. At that time, higher numbers of immigrants arrived at U.S. ports of entry and as America's own economy in some areas worsened, Congress began to pass immigration legislation. Ever since, the issue of immigration to the United States has drawn increased attention. In the field of criminology, there has also been increased attention to what has been called "crimmigration"—the area of law that is related to the nexus between immigration and criminal law (García Hernández, 2013; Ortega and Lasch, 2014; Sklansky, 2012; Stumpf, 2006). Immigration fraud has emerged as an important issue related to theorizing about crime and its causes, social context, and control. One type of immigration fraud that is the subject of growing interest is Green Card marriage fraud (i.e., a marriage between a non-U.S. citizen and a U.S. citizen, entered into for the sole purpose of obtaining a lawful permanent resident status in the United States by a non-U.S. citizen). Those who have been granted the privilege of residing permanently in the United States receive a document called "Permanent Resident Card," commonly referred to as the "Green Card." There are civil and criminal penalties under both the *Immigration and Nationality Act* (INA) and the *U.S. Criminal Code* for the commission of fraud in seeking a Green Card.

Little is known about this crime, the actors engaged in it, or its underlying and proximate causes. The original research completed for this book is designed to: explore and understand the experiences of individuals who participate in Green Card marriage fraud; to develop a better description of the crime; and to inform a theoretical model grounded in data that will contribute to understanding how and why immigrants and U.S. citizens engage in marriage fraud.

In order to legally enter or remain in the United States and be eligible for various immigration-related benefits, aliens must comply with a number of requirements. There is evidence that some persons engage in fraudulent actions to become eligible to obtain official documents (e.g., visas, Permanent Resident Cards, and Refugee Travel Documents) required to legally enter or remain in the United States (Lernatovych, 2014).

There are different ways to arrange a fraudulent marriage. This book focuses on one type called "cash-for-vows" where immigrants pay U.S. citizens for marriage in order to obtain resident status (for purposes of brevity, this type of crime is referred to as "Green Card marriage fraud"). Such fraud is not only more popular than other types but also easier for agents of the U.S. Citizenship and Immigration Services (USCIS) to identify as fraudulent. As soon as the fact of paying for the service is proven, the marriage is considered fraud. Thus, this act is clearly criminal, as the immigrant pays to illegally get access to benefits to which he/she is not entitled. Both the foreign spouse and the U.S. citizen knowingly participate in the criminal activity and both are lawbreakers.

The involvement of U.S. citizens weakens the nation's security system. In their brochure on immigration marriage fraud, Immigration and Custom Enforcement (ICE) indicates that this is a serious federal crime and states that participating U.S. citizens are "trading America's security for financial gain" (ICE, 2014b, p. 2). The citizens are viewed as knowingly or unknowingly aiding terrorists, foreign intelligence, or other criminal organizations (ICE, 2014b). Therefore, Green Card marriage fraud is not considered by authorities to be a victimless crime and its seriousness requires more attention from researchers.

On the other hand, the lawful issuance and receipt of Green Cards for immediate relatives of U.S. citizens serve the purpose of helping to reunite families, including married couples. However, the apparent ease of obtaining a permanent residency status based on marriage is also a mean of circumventing the standard immigration process.[1] Through an in-depth investigation into the crime of Green Card marriage fraud, the experiences of the people involved in it, and push factors encouraging the decision to participate in this fraudulent activity, this book aims to expand knowledge about the crime and present recommended changes to the immigration system as a way to address it.

The study of Green Card marriage fraud acquires special meaning at a time when continued growth of the immigrant population has resulted in many controversies including division in public opinion and continuous changes in the immigration system. Crime control and migration control have become so intertwined that they have ceased to be distinct processes that target distinct acts (Ortega and Lasch, 2014). The merging of immigration law and the U.S.

Criminal Code and penal system is called "crimmigration" by scholars in the field (García Hernández, 2013; Ortega and Lasch, 2014; Sklansky, 2012; Stumpf, 2006). The Green Card marriage fraud phenomenon falls in the intersection of immigration and crime, thus gaining significance for in-depth study. Despite the fact that, "the field of immigration studies is one of the most active and rich areas of social science," (Koff, 2008, p. 67), scholars have not sufficiently addressed the need to both explain the uniqueness of immigration cases and to build theory (Koff, 2008). The literature on immigration marriage fraud is very limited. If the topic is studied it is usually in relation to immigration law (Seminara, 2008)[2] or family law (Abrams, 2012; 2013), but no attempt has been made to understand the perceptions, perspectives, and experiences of people involved in Green Card marriage fraud (as participants or as "marriage fraud brokers"[3]). This research addresses two issues: explaining the uniqueness of such immigration case law and building theory.

This book explores the experiences of people who participated in Green Card marriage fraud and inform a new theoretical model grounded in data that may help explain why and how immigrants engage in marriage fraud. It seeks to add to the body of research by providing firsthand accounts of social, individual, and legal factors that are associated with the processes involved in this type of crime. Significantly, the broad patterns of a specific type of immigration marriage fraud called "cash-for-vows" and the role of marriage fraud brokers are identified and discussed.[3]

NOTES

1. Immigration status that allows non-U.S. citizens to live and work permanently in the United States. Aliens with permanent residency status receive a United States Permanent Resident Card (USCIS Form I-551), informally known as a Green Card.

2. Research published only on the Center for Immigration Studies website; not published in a peer-reviewed journal.

3. Marriage fraud brokers are those who are systematically arranging fraudulent marriages between immigrants and U.S. citizens for financial gain.

Part I

THE CRIMMIGRATION NEXUS

Chapter One

American Immigration Policy

In 1875, the Supreme Court ruled that regulating immigration is a federal responsibility. Before that, immigration policies were relatively flexible and welcoming. However, declining wages and economic problems on the West Coast began being attributed to Chinese workers. This resulted in the first significant law restricting immigration into the United States, the *Chinese Exclusion Act of 1882*. Shortly after, *Alien Contract Labor Laws of 1885* and *1887* were passed prohibiting any company or individual from bringing unskilled immigrants into the United States to work under contract (USCIS, 2019b).

The first immigration laws were enforced by state boards or commissions with direction from U.S. Treasury Department officials. "At the Federal level, U.S. Customs Collectors at each port of entry collected the head tax from immigrants while 'Chinese Inspectors' enforced the *Chinese Exclusion Act*" (USCIS, 2019b). Based on the *Immigration Act of 1891*, the federal government assumed direct control of inspecting, admitting, rejecting, and processing all immigrants seeking admission to the United States. The 1891 Act also created the Office of the Superintendent of Immigration within the Treasury Department that oversaw a new corps of U.S. Immigrant Inspectors stationed at the country's principal ports of entry. In 1895, the Office of Immigration was promoted to the Bureau of Immigration, and later in 1903 was transferred to the Department of Commerce and Labor (USCIS, 2019b).

At the beginning of the twentieth century, federal attention turned to standardizing naturalization procedures nationwide as the existing system lacked uniformity, resulting in widespread naturalization fraud. Congress responded to this issue by enacting the *Basic Naturalization Act of 1906*. This Act also created the Federal Naturalization Service, within the Bureau of Immigration and Naturalization structure, to oversee the nation's naturalization courts.

The United States experienced an ever increasing flow of immigrants during the early years of the twentieth century. Between 1900 and 1920, as the nation admitted over 14.5 million immigrants (USCIS, 2019b), Congress again strengthened its national immigration law. One of the novelties brought by the new *Immigration Act of 1917* was the requirement for all immigrants to be literate. A year later, passport requirements were imposed. Additionally, the Immigration Service began to issue Border Crossing Cards for Canadians and Mexicans. At the conclusion of World War I, the number of immigrants began to rapidly increase and Congress responded with the *Immigration Acts of 1921 and 1924*. These federal statutes introduced America's first quota system. "Each nationality received a quota based on its representation in past United States census figures. The State Department distributed a limited number of visas each year through U.S. Embassies abroad and the Immigration Service only admitted immigrants who arrived with a valid visa" (USCIS, 2019b).

More restrictive laws resulted in increased illegal immigration. In order to control it, in 1924 Congress created the U.S. Border Patrol within the Immigration Service. In 1933, the Bureau of Immigration and the Bureau of Naturalization reunited into a single agency, the Immigration and Naturalization Service (INS). Seven years later, INS was moved from the Department of Labor to the Department of Justice.

In 1952 Congress enacted the *Immigration and Nationality Act* (INA) codified under Title 8 of the U.S. Code (8 U.S.C. Ch. 12). It includes all previous immigration and naturalization laws. One of the crucial changes that this law brought was the abolishment of all racial restrictions found in U.S. immigration and naturalization statutes. However, the INA retained a quota system for nationalities and regions. Eventually, the Act established a preference system that determined which ethnic groups were desirable immigrants based mainly on family connections and labor qualifications.

The *Immigration Reform and Control Act* (IRCA) of 1986 expanded responsibilities of INS and also created an amnesty program giving those who have been "continuously physically present" in the United States since before January 1, 1982 an opportunity to legalize their residence.

The next important law, the *Immigration Act of 1990* (IMMACT 90) increased the number of available immigrant visas and revised the preference categories governing permanent legal immigration. Immigrant visas are now divided into three separate categories: family-sponsored, employment-based, and a diversity visa program that created a lottery to admit immigrants from "low admittance" countries or countries whose citizenry was underrepresented in the United States. This act also established an administrative procedure for naturalization and ended judicial naturalization. These new procedures empowered Federal Naturalization Examiners to grant or deny naturalization petitions.

Finally, the events of September 11, 2001, shifted the focus of American immigration law to border security and removal of criminal aliens to protect the nation from terrorist attacks. In 2003, the INS was abolished and its functions placed under three new federal agencies within the newly created Department of Homeland Security:

- Customs and Border Protection (CBP) that prevents drugs, weapons, and terrorists and other inadmissible persons from entering the country.
- Immigration and Customs Enforcement (ICE) that enforces criminal and civil laws governing border control, customs, trade, and immigration.
- U.S. Citizenship and Immigration Services (USCIS) to oversee lawful immigration to the United States and the naturalization of new American citizens (USCIS, 2019b).

This complex immigration system has an impact on the lives of 44,728,721 foreign-born people in the United States (U.S. Census Bureau, 2018a). The foreign-born population consists of 22,629,737 naturalized U.S. citizens and 22,098,984 non-U.S. citizens.[1] According to the most recent data (January 2015) collected by the Department of Homeland Security, 13,250,000 foreign born are legal permanent residents and 11,960,000 are unauthorized immigrants (Baker, 2018).[2] Moreover, during 2016, there were 186,200,000 nonimmigrant admissions to the United States, including tourists and business travelers, temporary workers and families, and students (DHS, 2018, Yearbook, Table 27). Many of these individuals want to stay in the country permanently, but since their permission to stay in the United States is just temporary, they are likely to seek avenues to officially extend their stay. Approximately two-thirds of new unauthorized arrivals in 2014 entered the United States on legal nonimmigrant visas and overstayed their visas' validity period (Warren and Kerwin, 2017). Some apply for visa extensions, some for permanent resident status, and others will overstay their authorized period and their existing nonimmigrant visa becomes automatically void.

The immigration system controls and regulates the composition and size of immigrant flow into the United States. Consequently, legal migration may not be an option available for everyone. In 2018, 63.4 percent of all immigrants who were able to obtain a Green Card did so through family members,[3] and within this category, 38 percent of Green Cards were issued to spouses of Americans (DHS, 2018, Table 6). For some people, these numbers expose weaknesses in the U.S. immigration system that must be addressed.

Green Card marriage fraud (GCMF) is often referred to as immigration marriage fraud. It is a fraudulent action that carries civil and criminal penalties under both the INA and the U.S. Criminal Code. Placement of the GCMF between branches of the law speaks to the uniqueness of its foundations. The intersection of criminal and civil law is described below and sheds light on the foundation of crimmigration.

There is no set definition of a GCMF—also called sham or fraudulent marriage. According to the ICE, it can only occur when a marriage is entered into for the sole purpose of gaining an immigration benefit. This definition can be also deduced from the law, which states that United States Citizenship and Immigration Services (USCIS) will deny an immigration petition if the alien has in the past, or is currently attempting or conspiring to, "enter into a marriage for the purpose of evading the immigration laws" (INA, Section 204(c)).

Uncovering sham marriages is a top priority of USCIS. During the immigration process, USCIS requires applicants to provide the evidence that their marriage is *bona fide*, or was entered into in "good faith." A marriage is entered into in good faith if the couple intended to establish a life together at the time of the marriage (*Bark v. INS*, 511 F.2d 1200, 1202 (9th Cir. 1975)). A finding of marriage fraud can have both civil and criminal consequences for the immigrant, and criminal consequences for the petitioner (U.S. citizens or Green Card holders who apply for a permanent residency for their spouses). Since marriage fraud is a federal crime, the consequences are severe. According to the *INA*,

> Any individual who knowingly enters into a marriage for the purpose of evading any provision of the immigration laws shall be imprisoned for not more than five years, or fined not more than $250,000, or both. (I.N.A. Section 275(c))

Additionally, a foreign national can be placed in the process of deportation based on 8 U.S. Code § 1227(a) (1) (G). If he or she still holds a nonimmigrant (temporary) visa, it can be revoked. The record of marriage fraud would remain on the person's immigration record forever, making it virtually impossible to obtain a Green Card in the future or even a nonimmigrant U.S. visa (ICE, 2014a). A person can also be convicted for violation of, or an attempt or a conspiracy to violate, section 1546 of title 18 (relating to fraud and misuse of visas, permits, and other entry documents, and making false statements under oath). The most severe punishment—not more than 25 years—can be applied if the offense was committed to facilitate an act of international terrorism; 20 years—if the offense was committed to facilitate a drug trafficking crime, and 10 years if the offense was not committed to facilitate such an act of international terrorism or a drug trafficking crime, or 15 years (in the case of any other offense), or both (18 U.S. Code § 1546).

Systematically arranging fraudulent marriages for financial gain is treated, by law, as engaging in conspiracy operations; hence, marriage fraud brokers who participate in this procedure can be subjected to the punishment of up to 25 years of incarceration. The U.S. Code states that:

> Any person who knowingly aids or assists any alien inadmissible under section 1182(a)(2) (insofar as an alien inadmissible under such section has been convicted of an aggravated felony) or 1182(a)(3) (other than subparagraph (E) thereof) of this title to enter the United States, or who connives or conspires with any person or persons to allow, procure, or permit any such alien to enter the United States, shall be fined under title 18, or imprisoned not more than 10 years, or both. (8 U.S. Code § 1327)

Although penalties for entering marriage for the sole purpose of obtaining legal residence in the United States and for arranging fraudulent marriages are severe, many people still decide to participate in this activity. It has been argued that this is mostly due to the fact that the U.S. immigration law offers only a few options to go from being an illegal immigrant to a U.S. permanent resident. One may be eligible to apply for a Green Card through family, a job offer or employment, refugee or asylum status, or a number of other special provisions, such as: religious worker, a child who has been abused, abandoned, or neglected by their parent, battered spouse or child (VAWA), Afghan/Iraqi translator, Afghan or Iraqi who assisted the U.S. government, armed forces member, international broadcaster, NATO-6 nonimmigrant, certain individuals from Cuba or Haiti, victim of criminal activity or trafficking, American Indian born in Canada, person born in the United States to a foreign diplomat, and more (USCIS, 2020a). A detailed description of all categories is attached in Appendix 1.

Despite the variety of ways to permanent residency, in 2018, 63.4 percent of all immigrants who obtained a Green Card did so through family members (DHS, 2018, Table 6). Under the U.S. immigration laws, those eligible based on this category are:

- An immediate relative of a U.S. citizen (spouses, unmarried children under the age of 21, and parents of U.S. citizen petitioners 21 or older).
- Other relative of a U.S. citizen (unmarried sons or daughters over the age of 21, married children of any age, and brothers and sisters of U.S. citizen petitioners 21 or older).
- Family member of a Green Card holder (spouses, unmarried sons or daughters over the age of 21, married children of any age).

- Fiancé(e) of a U.S. citizen or the fiancé(e)'s child.
- Widow(er) of a U.S. citizen.
- VAWA self-petitioner—victim of battery or extreme cruelty (USCIS, 2020a).

Within the family-sponsored category in 2018, 38.6 percent of Green Cards issued were to spouses of Americans. In 2018, 24.5 percent of all 1,096,611 immigrants who were granted permanent residency did so based on marriage with a U.S. citizen that made them "immediate relatives" (DHS, 2018, Table 7). As during previous reforms, one of the primary goals of the U.S. immigration was to reunite families, including married couples. According to the immigration policy, alien spouses should receive priority over all other immigration petitioners since alien spouses are in the immediate family category. The goal of the policy is to keep immediate families together, by providing a higher priority status in comparison to petitioners who do not fall into this category (Padgett Torres, 2014). However, the apparent ease of obtaining a Green Card based on marriage has led to abuse. Couples regularly enter into sham marriage—the U.S. citizen engaging in the marriage in exchange for money or other benefits, foreigners for immigration benefits. In *Lutwak et al. v. United States* (344 U.S. 604 (1953)), the Supreme Court stated that "Congress did not intend to provide aliens with an easy means of circumventing the quota system by fake marriages in which neither of the parties ever intended to enter into the marital relationship. . . " This unresearched form of crime should attract the attention of researchers and experts in order to explain why this particular category is the most popular.

As mentioned above, there is no set definition of a sham marriage; however, the U.S. Code gives a frame to build a definition. According to 8 USC § 1325c, "Any individual who knowingly enters into a marriage for the purpose of evading any provision of the immigration laws shall be imprisoned for not more than 5 years, or fined not more than $250,000, or both."

Moreover, the U.S. Code refers to marriage fraud by stating that:

> An alien shall be considered to be deportable as having procured a visa or other documentation by fraud (within the meaning of section 1182 (a)(6)(C)(i) of this title) and to be in the United States in violation of this chapter (within the meaning of subparagraph (B)) if—
>
> (i) The alien obtains any admission into the United States with an immigrant visa or other documentation procured on the basis of a marriage entered into less than 2 years prior to such admission of the alien and which, within 2 years subsequent to any admission of the alien in the United States, shall be judicially annulled or terminated, unless the alien establishes to the satisfaction of the Attorney General that such marriage was not contracted for the purpose of evading any provisions of the immigration laws

(ii) It appears to the satisfaction of the Attorney General that the alien has failed or refused to fulfill the alien's marital agreement which in the opinion of the Attorney General was made for the purpose of procuring the alien's admission as an immigrant. (8 USC § 1227)

In simple words, marriage fraud can only occur when a marriage is entered into for the sole purpose of gaining an immigration benefit. However, that determination is often left up to an immigration official and it is the responsibility of the applicant to prove that the marriage was entered into in good faith. There are many ways to arrange a fraud marriage. The current research focuses only on the type called "cash-for-vows" (where immigrants pay Americans for marriage), which for the purpose of this research is called simply "Green Card marriage."

Immigration has been both a burden and essential building block for the United States. Undoubtedly, American culture and economy have been shaped by people from around the world. Many specialists highlight the fact that immigration has been vital to the economic growth of the country (Hanson, 2012). For example, immigrants are creating and preserving U.S. manufacturing jobs and making once-declining areas more attractive to the U.S.-born population (Killawi, 2013; Vigdor, 2013).[4] However, in the opinion of many Americans, those who enter the United States illegally or extend their stay in violation of immigration law endanger national security (Time, 2006) and cause many other problems such as: crime; increase use of social services; adding to overpopulation in cities; hurting Americans by competing with them for jobs; and driving down wages.

Historically, no country has been more closely bound to immigration than the United States. Generally, the costs and benefits of immigration continue to be the subject of many academic and public debates (López-Sander, 2014). The debate over the costs and benefits of immigration led to an evolution and a change of attitude toward foreign-born people. Today, Americans are divided into those who support free immigration movements and those who hope to limit immigration. Despite current public opinion in regard to immigration, there is still a strong economic demand for the cheap disposable labor foreign workers deliver. Such ambivalence on these issues has changed the nature of immigration policy. Trujillo-Pagan, N. (2014) calls this phenomenon the U.S. "immigration complex."

Some have argued that the changing nature of immigration policy has shifted the U.S. system of immigration control to a system of "crimmigration" that has a very negative impact on the lives of many foreign-born people (those with and without legal status) (Ortega and Lasch, 2014). Also, aliens face numerous unique challenges relating to their current and evolving legal status,[5] socioeconomic situation, and psychosocial well-being. Those

aliens who do not have permanent legal residency may seek opportunities to
improve their situation through legitimizing their stay in the United States.
The Green Card, the awarding of which permits legal residency and generally
places an immigrant on a steady path toward American citizenship, is a critical tool that immigrants can use to avoid the negative impacts associated with
crimmigration policies. For some, the only real chance of achieving security
and permanence in the United States is by engaging in GCMF that makes
them immediate relatives of U.S. citizens and, as such, legitimate members
of American society.

Global inequality, whether in terms of wages, labor market and educational
opportunities, or lifestyles, results in a constantly increasing flow of migrants
into the United States (Black, Natali, and Skinner, 2006). This pattern will
likely continue. People move across borders, seeking to reduce what they see
as the gap between their own position and that of people in more developed
countries.

Migration—the movement of people to countries different than countries
where they were born, with the intentions of temporarily or permanently set-
tling in order to find better living conditions—is a complex process. There
are many reasons why people choose to migrate. However, the basic driving
forces are economic and political. Economic migration is usually explained
as the result of a cost-benefit analysis. Many researchers argue that main
determinants of migration flows are rooted in the differential between the
economic situations in the home and host countries (in terms of incomes,
unemployment, inequalities, poverty, education levels, etc.) and migration
costs (Harris and Todaro, 1970; Naiditch, Tomini, and Ben Lakhdar, 2015).
Foreigners residing in the United States are often responsible for their families in their countries of origin. Remittances from immigrants supplement
the incomes of those who remain behind. This is an important push factor to
make a decision regarding migration (Drachman and Paulino, 2004; Naiditch,
Tomini, and Ben Lakhdar, 2015).

Some immigrants come with hopes of reunification with a family member
currently residing in the United States. This process is informally called chain
migration.

President Donald J. Trump sought to move from a current largely family-
based immigration system toward a more merit-based structure. On August
2nd, 2017, President Trump announced the *Reforming American Immigration
for Strong Employment* (RAISE) *Act*.[6] "This bill eliminates the diversity visa
program, replaces the current employment visa system with a skills-based
point system, eliminates certain family-based immigration preferences, and
establishes a 50,000 annual limit for refugees given permanent resident status" (U.S. Senate, S.1720). Under the proposed merit-based visa category,

immigrants would accrue points based on a holistic assessment of their age, education, extraordinary achievements, job offer, English language proficiency, business activities, and ties to the United States.

Merit-based systems could be potentially beneficial for immigrants who currently see GCMF as their only option to Legal Permanent Residency in the United States. Although assessment of chances of GCMF participants to qualify for visa or Legal Permanent Residency based on the *RAISE Act* is beyond the scope of this research, it is noteworthy that considering age, education, job status, English language proficiency,[7] and ties to the United States of interviewed immigrants, the majority of them would have a chance to qualify. By using merit-based points systems and assigning weights to different factors, the United States would signal to the world the required characteristics needed by future immigrants. Those who strongly desire to live permanently in the United States would get a chance to work on certain characteristics that would help them to collect more points and increase their chances of qualifying for a visa or a Green Card. The merit-based system could potentially help to reduce the number of fraud marriages for immigration purposes by simply providing a pathway to Legal Permanent Residency to those who previously felt stripped from options other than GCMF.

There are other important reasons why individuals are forced to or want to migrate from their home countries to the United States. Such reasons may include armed conflict, social strife, and political turmoil. Beyond wars, government persecution of political opponents, human rights violations, and ethnic cleansing campaigns (called "domestic" politics) may have far-reaching effects on increasing the number of migrants (Salehyan, 2008).

However, when immigrants arrive on American soil (irrespectively of their status), they face numerous unique challenges. Change of country and residency always requires acculturation (Bornstein and Bohr, 2011). Undocumented immigrants face multiple levels of inequality, including those that arise from their racial and class status (Gleeson and Gonzales, 2012). Many are also subjected to prejudice and discrimination when they differ from the general population in terms of language, religion, physical appearance, and socioeconomic status (Rumbaut and Ewing, 2007).

One of the most difficult aspects of immigration is finding employment. Access to many opportunities like higher-paid jobs, college education, or health insurance may be restricted to U.S. citizens and lawful permanent residents only.

An appreciation of the determinants of immigration remains crucial for a general understanding of the distinctive aspects regarding immigration in the United States. Moreover, the immigrant population in the United States is still increasing, irrespective of its complex factors, uniqueness, and challenges.

NOTES

1. Size of foreign-born population was estimated base on the U.S. Census data for 2018, which is the most current year available. Numbers of legal permanent residents and unauthorized immigrants are estimated base on data provided by the Department of Homeland Security for 2015, which is the most current data available. For consistency, according to the U.S. Census in 2015 the foreign-born population was 44,290,372.

2. The totals provided by U.S. Census and Department of Homeland Security are different because U.S. Census data has been augmented and adjusted to account for an undercount of the population.

3. This number is based on a combination of two categories of admission: the family-sponsored preferences category involving 216,563 admissions (19.7 percent) and the immediate relatives of U.S. citizens category involving 478,961 admissions (43.7 percent). In 2018 a total of 1,096,611 immigrants obtained lawful permanent resident status.

4. According to Vigdor's (2013) research, that included 3,100 counties, for every 1,000 immigrants that arrive to a county, 270 U.S.-born residents also move there in response. "These residents are drawn by the increasing demand for service-oriented businesses ranging from restaurants to law firms and by the employment that is preserved in sectors like manufacturing" (Vigdor, 2013, p. 3).

5. Non-U.S. citizens.

6. S.1720—RAISE Act—115th Congress (2017–2018), Sponsor: Sen. Cotton, Tom [R-AR] (Introduced 08/02/2017), read twice and referred to the Committee on the Judiciary. Full text available at: https://www.congress.gov/bill/115th-congress/senate -bill/1720/text?q=%7B%22search%22%3A%5B%22raise+act%22%5D%7D&r=1.

7. Based on the quality of the communication during the interview, the interviewer can make a statement that all interviewed immigrants speak English fluently.

Chapter Two

Macro and Micro View on the Intersection of Crime and Immigration

When studying immigrants' issues, it is useful to look at all factors that may influence their unique situation on both the macro and micro levels. The macro level consists of the broad socioeconomic and political factors. The micro level encompasses the individual, family, and local community-related factors.

At the macro level, there is a strong link between poverty and immigration. Immigrants in the United States who do not have a work permit face a variety of problems that often lead to diminished financial opportunities. Primary causes of this situation include underemployment, unemployment, low wages, and restricted mobility. In addition, the vast majority of immigrants come from countries with higher poverty levels than the United States (U.S. Census, 2018a). Due to both their previous fragile economic condition in the country of origin and their unstable situation in United States, immigrants in general have lower incomes than native-born Americans. According to the U.S. Census (2018b), 8.1 percent of native families have incomes that place them below the poverty line, while for non-U.S. citizen families this number grows to 18.4 percent. Additionally, immigrants who are not U.S. citizens are more than twice as likely to live in poverty (23 percent) than immigrants who have been naturalized as U.S. citizens (10 percent). For some groups of immigrants, the impact is greater. For example, Hispanic immigrant poverty rates are nearly double that of other immigrants (Sullivan and Ziegert, 2008). Thus, many immigrants desperately look for the way to get out of poverty; many see the chance to achieve it through a Green Card marriage.

The analysis of the macro level factors related to Green Card marriage fraud (GCMF) should start from an overview of the legitimization process of the state in decisions about rules of inclusion and exclusions of its members. One approach to this analysis is an exploration of the very limited language available to describe different ways of defining people's membership to the community. Thomas Hammar (1990) categorizes this deficit in a discussion of "denizenship"—referring to those who are not citizens and thus are not full members of the society but who are not "foreigners" either. Despite lacking citizenship, denizens typically have substantial rights in their countries of residence, but not a formal membership. In democratic systems, the legitimacy of the state is derived from the notion that the government represents the will of the people. The will of the people is expressed via active and passive voting rights (Bartram, Poros, and Monforte, 2014). This conceptualization suggests that even if immigrants do not have a status in the United States, they play a role in the legitimation process of the state they live in. Immigrants who are not citizens of a state may still have a direct relationship with the state, especially by the nature of their long-term physical presence in that space. They are subjected to rules and systems of control in the state where they reside. Jo Shaw (2007) argues, "the ascription of citizenship (to some and not to others) could be seen to be recognition of inequality or at least difference" (p. 20). Immigrants have the same rules and the same responsibilities as citizens while having significantly fewer rights and benefits. Based on the absence of national political rights, denizenship becomes a status of vulnerability to domination (in both private and public sectors).

Stumpf's (2006) membership theory explains how individual rights and privileges are limited to the members of a social contract between the government and the people. Some individuals are included in the social contract and others excluded from it. In regard to immigrants, the state decides who is permitted to live in the United States, who is awarded membership to the U.S. population and who is to be expelled from this society. However, those alienated and excluded may not simply accept denied membership but rather may look for avenues to inclusion; for some this avenue is Green Card marriage.

Denied many rights, noncitizens (and especially those who are not legal residents) constitute a group similar to second-class citizens. According to Pope and Garrett (2012), "the illegal immigrant is more than marginalized—They are effectively and legally neutralized" (p. 175). Undocumented immigrants have been described as *Homo Sacer* because they are "set apart," seen as outside of the normal juridical space, excluded from all rights and privileges of a citizen (Pope and Garrett, 2012). Hence, it should not be a surprise that some are ready to do whatever they can to move from the "illegal" to "legal" zone.

Using the dual lens of Agamben's (1995) "state of exception theory" and *Homo Sacer* theory, Pope and Garrett (2012) examine U.S. immigration policy, deportation policy, and border security. The "state of exception theory" has its roots in the French revolution and was popular in the mid-twentieth century as the "paradigmatic form of government." This theory is similar to a state of emergency, however derived from the sovereign's ability to transcend the rule of law in the name of the public good.[1] In other words, state of exception is the expansion of executive power in response to existential threats to the nation, such as "war on terror."[2] This theory explains the extra space carved out to justify legal exceptions. Immigrants who are not legally permitted to stay in the United States are not sovereign; they are outside of the normal juridical space, and thus, called *Homo Sacer*. As Agamben (1995) recalls based on Roman law, *Homo Sacer* is the sacred (as in the meaning of the word as set apart) or accused man who is banned and may be killed by anyone but not sacrificed. Unlike legal citizens, *Homo Sacer* is excluded from all rights and privileges. This concept can be applied to current undocumented immigrants in the United States, excluding the aspect of "being killed by anyone."

> The exception created within the legal mechanisms of the state power causes Homo Sacer to be both controlled and excluded simultaneously within the process of government. The illegal immigrant within the American system of both entry and citizenship equally fits this definition as the banned individual under Roman law. (Pope and Garrett, 2012, p. 174)

Laws like the *USA Patriot Act* and the *Real ID Act* further separate immigrants with legal and no legal statuses, therefore diminishing rights of those with no legal status. The legal power of the people as sovereign is derived from their legal status as U.S. citizens. Hence, undocumented immigrants can be easily deprived of many basic human rights. The fight for those rights and individual legitimacy can become a life goal for many immigrants. That is where the marriage fraud becomes useful, or viewed by some as a necessity. Powerlessness causes frustration, and frustrated people are more likely to commit crimes. This sense of *Homo Sacer* may apply not only to immigrants but also to other vulnerable populations such as females (Carlen, 1990) or young African Americans (Messerschmidt, 1993).

This negative state feeds into the crimmigration phenomenon. American citizens increasingly perceive immigrants as "criminal aliens" instead of hard working foreigners coming to the United States for a better life. This process may be especially relevant in regard to the largest minority population in the United States—Latinos. They had been seen as a valuable source of unskilled labor that was very important for the American economy (Vazquez, 2015). Now they are equated with criminal offenders. Stumpf (2006) explains that:

> As criminal sanctions for immigration related conduct and criminal grounds for removal from the United States continue to expand, aliens become synonymous

with criminals. As collateral sanctions for criminal violations continue to target the hallmarks of citizenship and community membership, ex-offenders become synonymous with aliens.[3] (p. 419)

García Hernández (2015) argues that immigration enforcement has come to resemble criminal law enforcement. Acts that were previously civil violations are now criminal, and others carry penalties more severe than before (Miller, 2003). Increasing criminalization of immigration law is clearly visible when analyzing the issue of illegal entry into the United States. According to the *Immigration and Nationality Act* (INA),[4] illegal entry, which in immigration law is referred to as "improper entry by alien," is punishable by either fine, imprisonment up to six months, or both for first time offenders. According to the case of *Lewis v. United States* (8 U.S. Code §1325; I.N.A. Sec. 275), this act can be classified as a petty misdemeanor.[5] After being prosecuted for immigration violations, the immigrant will most likely be removed from the United States (deported) on the basis of a conviction as "criminal alien." For a subsequent offense, classified as "reentry of removed aliens," immigrants can be fined or imprisoned for up to two years, or both (8 U.S. Code §1326; I.N.A. Sec. 275). In cases of subsequent attempts of reentry to the United States (successfully or not), section 276 of INA provides a broad spectrum of punishments including imprisonment from two to 20 years (depending on circumstances). This example shows a very systematic criminalization effort over undocumented immigrants. According to ICE statistics from 2013, over 68 percent of all removals were based on criminal convictions for one of three crime categories: dangerous drugs, criminal traffic offenses, and immigration violations (TRAC Immigration, 2014). Social perception of "criminal aliens" has also been shaped by increased participation of local law enforcement officials in controlling and detaining immigrants through programs like Secure Communities (García Hernández, 2013; Ortega and Lasch, 2014).[6]

Between crimes committed by foreign-born individuals and current events, "Americans" fear of terrorist activities takes a high priority. Some analysts suggest that terrorist attacks (those attempted and those successfully carried out) provide evidence of the continuing threat to the United States by foreign-born legal immigrants (Haberfeld and Lieberman, 2012). Particular areas, such as the U.S.-Mexican border, are treated as gateways to potential criminal activities including terrorism and narco-terrorism. Ordinary Mexican workers are now treated as terror suspects (Arnold, 2007). The perceived emergency threat led to changes in federal and state legislation prioritizing immigration as a national security issue. This resulted in the creation of a connection between undocumented workers and the war on terror that has only served to enhance the distinction between the documented and the undocumented immigrants (Pope and Garrett, 2012).

On April 8, 2014, the Transactional Records Access Clearinghouse (TRAC) Immigration issued a report which looked at deportations carried out by ICE. According to this report, in 2013, almost 59 percent of these deportations were of immigrants with criminal convictions. However, this number needs to be further analyzed to unfold the truth that hides the crimmigration nexus. ICE uses extremely broad definitions of criminal behavior that include even the most minor violations. The "convicted criminal" category applies, inter alia, to traffic violations (like speeding) and drug offenses. In 2013, within the group of 368,644 deportees, 216,810 had criminal convictions. A total of 54,812 were convicted for the immigration crime of "illegal entry"; 47,249 convicted of traffic offenses, and 41,335 drug offenses. A total of 73,414 of others were convicted for other crimes like assault, larceny, burglary, etc. Hence, almost 59 percent of all removals were based on criminal convictions for one of these three crime categories (TRAC Immigration, 2014). Golash-Boza (2015) highlights that "deporting undocumented workers, traffic viola-tors, and drug users and sellers does not make America any less susceptible to terrorist attack" (p. 10), which is one of the biggest public concerns. Despite the evidence, Americans still believe immigrants are more likely than natives to commit crimes. Fear of crime is consistently and positively correlated with an unfavorable attitude of U.S. citizens toward immigrants (Bucerius and Tonry, 2014).

Marginalization, vulnerability to domination, and exclusion cause major difficulties in the lives of many foreigners residing in the United States. Their consequences spread beyond socioeconomic and political areas of life. They form basic building blocks for the development of further problems on the micro level, such as mental health, employment, education, family life, and functioning as a part of the community.

IMMIGRATION AND CRIME—MICRO VIEW

On the micro level, several factors affect the quality of life of immigrants, those with legal and no legal status. These may become direct push- or pull-factors in the individual's and family's process of deciding to engage in GCMF. A Green Card comes with several benefits that may significantly improve one's quality of life. Many scholars have pointed out that legal sta-tus is often the single most important determinant of benefits accessibility to immigrants. Benefits such as food stamps, unemployment compensation, health insurance, and public housing assistance (Bloemraad, 2006; Gleeson and Gonzales, 2012; Portes and Rumbaut, 2006; Reitz, 1998) are reserved for U.S. citizens and legal permanent residents. But a Green Card gives more

than financial assistance. Some of the most important benefits are freedom
of movement,[7] ability to sponsor relatives to come and live permanently
in the United States,[8] and after a certain number of years (usually three or
five), eligibility to apply for U.S. citizenship through naturalization (USCIS,
2020a). Although systematic assessment of factors affecting the life of immigrants in the United States is beyond the scope of this research the role these
push- and pull-factors play in GCMF, as described by several participants, is
considered.

The experiences of immigrants (those with legal status as well as those undocumented) in the United States affect their adjustment to life in this country. They face numerous unique challenges relating to their socioeconomic
situation and psychosocial well-being. One of the most difficult aspects of
immigration is finding employment. Even in light of recent data showing
that the unemployment rate of the foreign-born is 5.6 percent compared to
the native-born Americans unemployment rate at 6.3 percent (Bureau of
Labor Statistics, 2015), immigrants still struggle with unemployment and
underemployment. Many immigrants are educated and possess high-level
qualifications and/or years of professional experience that unfortunately cannot be transferred to the U.S. job market. Transferring from the high-skill to
low-skill job sector may increase stress and have a negative impact on one's
psychological well-being.

Foreign-born workers are more likely than native-born workers to fill low-
skilled jobs. They are more likely to be employed in service occupations (24.1
percent versus 16.4 percent); in production, transportation, and material moving occupations (15.6 percent versus 11.2 percent); and in natural resources,
construction, and maintenance occupations (13.7 percent versus 8.4 percent).
Consequently, they are less likely to be employed in high-skill jobs such as
management, professional, and related occupations (30.7 percent versus 39.8
percent) as well as sales and office occupations (16.0 percent versus 24.2
percent) (Bureau of Labor Statistics, 2015). According to Ji and Batalova
(2012), college-educated immigrants are more likely to be unemployed than
native-born Americans. Immigrants with legal status but without work permits and immigrants without legal status share similar employment-related
experiences. Employers in need of low skill and low wage employees are
more likely to give jobs to immigrants without proper work authorizations.
Many foreigners feel trapped in this underemployment cycle. Despite this difficult situation, most undocumented immigrants continue to "pay federal and
sales taxes, work at undesirable jobs for low wages, and live in areas where
many Americans would not reside" (Porter, 2006).

The Immigration Reform and Control Act (IRCA), passed in 1986, prohibits
an employer from knowingly hiring, recruiting, or referring illegal aliens for

work in the United States, whether or not they are unauthorized to work (but authorized to remain in the United States) or their stay in the United States is unauthorized. The law also extends to employers who discover that an employee is an illegal alien after hiring them. Furthermore, it is illegal for employers not to verify work authorization. Under federal law, three days after an employee is hired, employers should correctly complete an I-9 form (Employment Eligibility Verification). Failing to do so will subject employers to criminal and civil punishment (DHS, 2014). Therefore, most employers resist employing undocumented immigrants. Some decide to employ such workers but do so without registering that worker and pay him/her in cash only.

The impact of unequally distributed earnings for immigrants and non-immigrants may also apply to differentials for those with and without legal status. Chi and Drewianka (2014) try to estimate "How much is a Green Card worth?" for immigrants. They found consistent evidence that Mexican-born men with Green Cards earn about 30 percent more than they would without one. Lack of Green Cards causes the inability to secure the wage growth and inability to freely change jobs. Workers on visas (with work permissions) are usually tied to one employer only. Chi and Drewianka (2014) explain:

> workers allowed to work only in a specific occupation (or even for a particular employer) may be unable to secure the wage growth that often comes from actual or potential job mobility, and their inability to move may preclude the formation of more efficient employment matches. (p. 103)

During the present COVID-19 pandemic, some doctors, nurses, and other health care workers have been prevented from volunteering because of their immigration status. On April 18, 2020, NPR's Scott Simon spoke with Dr. Ram Alur, president of Physicians for American Healthcare Access, about restrictions faced by some immigrant doctors who want to help fight the pandemic. Dr. Ram Alur himself has been practicing medicine in the United States for 13 years under an H-1B visa and wanted to volunteer to work in New York City,[9] where, he thought, his service is most needed. Unfortunately his work permit restricts him to his employer in Marion, Illinois. Dr. Alur says *"We wanted to participate—there are thousands of physicians like me—and we are held back"* (Simon, 2020). This current situation illustrates how strict visa restrictions are and how they limit labor mobility.

In general, immigrants whose wages have been most affected by their inability to seek alternative employment have the strongest incentive to seek U.S. citizen-spouses who can help them become permanent residents. In the same research, Chi and Drewianka (2014) also raise the issue of intermarriage premiums that may pose additional incentive to engage in a marriage fraud.[10]

Many immigrants treat the Green Card as an investment, and carefully calculate potential benefits and risks that GCMF may carry.

A Green Card can help immigrants to battle problems linked to employment and the financial stability that comes with it. According to USCIS (2020), a Green Card can be used for two main purposes:

- To prove employment eligibility in the United States when completing the Form I-9, Employment Eligibility Verification.
- To apply for a Social Security Card and a state-issued driver's license. In other words, a Green Card gives immigrants freedom to live in the United States permanently, and to work for any employer, regardless of job position or number of work hours within a week. Permanent residents do not need an employer sponsorship comparable to visa holders and may change employers whenever and wherever they may want.

Studies have shown an association between underemployment (in regard to perceived skills utilization) and lower levels of psychological well-being (Johnson, Morrow, and Johnson, 2002; Kahn and Morrow, 1991; Maynard, Joseph, and Maynard, 2006). Some researchers use a term "brain waste" to describe this trend where immigrants who were highly skilled professionals in their home countries become stymied in their efforts to find highly-skilled employment in the United States. Such skilled employment may have been at the same or at least similar level to what they had in their home countries based on their education, talents, training, and/or professional experience (Batalova, McHugh, and Morawski, 2014). For many, their only hope is to obtain a Green Card in order to be able to compete for better employment opportunities. Some states require U.S. citizenship or Green Cards to be eligible for professional licenses, such as real estate or insurance agent. In professions such as law enforcement or security, employees must be eligible to obtain a firearm license. Immigrants are generally not eligible, unless they are Green Card holders. With a Green Card, a foreign-born person can own firearms (18 U.S.C. 922 (d) (5), (g) (5)). Moreover, permanent residents can also start their own businesses and create their own corporations. A great advantage of Green Card holders over visa holders with work authorization is that some jobs require security clearances that only Green Card holders and U.S. citizens can apply for. Thus, a Green Card provides more (and often better) job opportunities. It has also been reported that many companies, government agencies, high-security labs, and programs employ only U.S. citizens or Green Card holders, and so do not accept applicants holding visas even when they are authorized to work in the U.S. (National Research Council, 2005). Immigrants without legal status to work and reside in the United States may not see the chance to improve their employment-related situation. This, in turn, may cause lower levels of psychological well-being and may push an immigrant toward the decision to engage in illegal activity, like marriage fraud.

Education is another push factor that may contribute to the decision regarding entering Green Card marriage. In 1982, the Supreme Court ruled in *Plyler v. Doe* (457 U.S. 202) that children are "persons" protected by the Due Process Clauses of the Fifth and Fourteenth Amendments, and as such, states may not deny them access to public education regardless of their legal status. However, the Court's decision did not extend to higher education. Also, immigrants face structural barriers such as a lack of adequate mentoring, limited information on eligibility from postsecondary institutions, and most importantly, financial burden (Baum and Flores, 2011). They are not eligible for financial aid, scholarships, fellowships, or even on-campus employment. As a result, many immigrants cannot afford to go to college. A Green Card can change their situation because permanent residents have a right to apply for government-sponsored aid for education and are eligible for in-state tuition (U.S. Department of Education, 2012). Also, graduate students may be attracted by eligibility to apply for government research grants that are not available for while being visa holders (Wasem, 2014).

Moreover, parents' unauthorized residency status in the United States. may keep children in poverty and unstable living arrangements because the parents may be too fearful of deportation to claim even the public benefits for which their children qualify (Landale, Thomas, and Van Hook, 2011). A successful GCMF may open a new avenue to public benefits.

Economic and social insecurity that come with having no legal status can affect not only children in the family but also spouses or partners. Counts, Brown, and Campbell (1999) classify stress as a factor that increases the risk of perpetrating intimate partner violence. Some scholars have added economic mobility and uncertainty about future legal status to the list of risk factors caused by immigration status (Abraham, 2000)—the latter is particularly important to consider in understanding people married for the sole purpose of obtaining legal residence in the United States.

GCMFs also affect areas of life outside of the criminal law, including effects on family. If family structure is weakened, the well-being of family members is at risk, and the possibility of involvement in criminal activity increases (Ikäheimo et al., 2013). In this context, family law scholars suggest that lawmakers should reconsider how certain benefits are tied to marriage and disaggregate the components of marriage to which public benefits are attached (Abrams, 2012). This disaggregation would lead to fairer allocation and effective distribution of public benefits without the harm to the institution of marriage. There is a clear intersection between family law and immigration law. Marriage, as a central component of family life, should not be studied independently, without reference to the whole family. Likewise, family should always be studied as a social system. Abrams (2012) argues that if society becomes accustomed to the idea of marrying purely to receive benefits, then the idea that marriage is an important commitment to another person could become diluted over time. Edmonston (1996) suggests that no topic requires more systematic attention than family and social networks. To really understand living conditions of foreigners in the United States, as well as causes and determinants of decisions that they make in relation to immigration, all aspects of family life need to be studied before, during, and after immigration. Green Card marriage has already left its imprint on society. The problem is on the rise; therefore, increased negative influences can be expected.

NOTES

1. According to Agamben (1995), the Nazi concentration camps of World War II constitute the "state of exception." The author comments on the tragedy of mass extermination as follows: "Insofar as its inhabitants were stripped of every political status and wholly reduced to bare life, the camp was also the most absolute biopolitical space ever to have been realized, in which power confronts nothing but pure life, without any mediation" (p. 171).

2. Agamben (2005) used examples of stretching executive power by presidents Abraham Lincoln, Franklin D. Roosevelt, and George W. Bush to explain the destructive power of the "state of exception." He presents how the rule of law is routinely displaced by the "state of exception," or emergency declaration, subjecting groups to extra-judicial state violence. Also, current president of the United States Donald Trump (although not described by Agamben in his books) could be an example of implementation of state of emergency rules when signing his executive actions under the pretense of "war on terror" or "prioritizing national security." See also especially: https://immigrationforum.org/article/immigration-related-executive-actions-during -the-covid-19-pandemic/.

3. According to Stumpf (2006), immigrants are treated by the legal system similarly to ex-offenders. When a U.S. citizen commits a relatively serious crime and, as an effect, is incarcerated, he or she is stripped from critical elements of citizenship, such as: the ability to freely socialize with other community members, the right to exercise basic political rights (right to vote, serve in public office, or serve on a jury), and the ability to exercise social and welfare rights and benefits open to other citizens (e.g., financial assistance). The resulting status of an ex-offender resembles that of an immigrant who can be deported even for a minor offense. Once permanent residents or other legal residents are deported, their membership is effectively revoked (usually forever but a minimum of 10 years) and the person is removed from the society. In

cases of undocumented immigrants, this effect is even more severe because they are experiencing effects of revoked membership while still living in the United States, surrounded by legal members of the society. There are many similarities between ex-offenders and undocumented immigrants, for example, both groups cannot vote (in the case of ex-offenders it depends on what state they live in); serve in public office, or serve on a jury; bear arms or own guns; apply for federal or state grants; live in public housing; receive federal cash assistance, Supplemental Security Income (SSI) or food stamps, among other benefits. Moreover, they are prohibited from getting employment in certain fields. Another example that exposes similarities between these two groups is the Affordable Care Act's (ObamaCare) Health Insurance Marketplace. According to the website http://obamacarefacts.com, "The following groups aren't eligible to use the marketplace, get cost assistance, or use Medicaid or CHIP: Undocumented immigrants; Those who are currently incarcerated." Only these two groups are excluded.

4. "(a) Any alien who (1) enters or attempts to enter the United States at any time or place other than as designated by immigration officers, or (2) eludes examination or inspection by immigration officers, or (3) attempts to enter or obtains entry to the United States by a willfully false or misleading representation or the willful concealment of a material fact, shall, for the first commission of any such offense, be fined under title 18 or imprisoned not more than 6 months, or both, and, for a subsequent commission of any such offense, be fined under title 18, or imprisoned not more than 2 years, or both" (8 U.S. Code § 1325(a)).

5. "An offense carrying a maximum term of six months or less is presumed petty (. . .)" (Held, 1.).

6. Secure Communities is a federal immigration enforcement program being implemented by U.S. Immigration and Customs Enforcement (ICE). The program was created with the goal of improving the removal of unauthorized immigrants convicted of crime, with a priority on removing violent offenders. It has faced criticism over whether participation is voluntary or mandatory for states and localities, and whether it is meeting its objective of prioritizing dangerous or violent criminals for deportation. As a result, the Secure Communities program was discontinued in 2014. However, on January 25, 2017, the program was restarted by the Department of Homeland Security per an executive order signed by President Donald Trump (Executive Order 13768, titled Enhancing Public Safety in the Interior of the United States).

7. Green Card holders can leave the United States and come back at any time, without additional permits. However, this freedom is bounded by a single rule: the amount of time outside the United States cannot be longer than one year. Absence of a permanent resident in the country for over six months can be treated as abandonment of legal residency and result in rejection of readmission to the United States (USCIS, 2020a).

8. Eligible family members' category includes Green Card holder's spouse and unmarried child(ren) of any age. However, Congress has limited the number of relatives who may immigrate under these categories each year, which causes long waiting periods (USCIS, 2020a).

9. This type of visa allows U.S. employers to temporarily employ foreign workers in specialty occupations.

10. Intermarriage premiums defined as the gap in wages, earnings, or employment between intermarried (foreigner and U.S. citizen) and endogamous immigrants (two foreigners).

Chapter Three

Enforcement Aspects of Green Card Marriage Fraud

There are many ways to arrange a fraudulent marriage. Seminara (2008) describes a few of the most popular: mail order bride arrangements (where foreign brides can be picked by Americans from catalogs published online by companies that run international matchmaking businesses, solely for the purpose of obtaining a Green Card); phony "arranged" marriages (where parents choose spouses for their children); "cash-for-vows" (where immigrants pay Americans for marriage); friends-and-family plans (where someone pitches in to help get someone else's spouse to the United States); "I do, I don't, I do" marriages (where foreigners divorce their real spouses; marry Americans for two years and divorce them to remarry their original spouses to bring them to the United States); pop-up marriages for visa lottery winners, exploitative relationships (where the foreigner is exploited in some way or abused); and heartbreakers (where foreigners dupe Americans into believing their love is real, when they just want a Green Card).

According to the Center for Immigration Studies, mail order bride arrangements, phony "arranged" marriages, and friends-and-family plans are much harder to detect and prove as fraudulent because spouses are more likely to live together and act as real spouses than in the case of "cash-for-vows" marriages. Moreover, these marriages usually involve family and friends, which creates additional proof of the legitimacy of the marriage (witnesses, pictures that involve other people). "Cash-for-vows" and heartbreakers are the two most common ways to enter sham-marriage (Seminara, 2008; Lernatovych, 2014), and they should be given a closer look. According to a USCIS officer (interview, 2012), with regard to heartbreakers the problem is more complicated because American spouses genuinely believe that their relationships are real and based on mutual affection. Despite the evidence showing otherwise, they trust that their foreign partners love them. This kind of activity is based on feelings and emotions, hence it is very hard to detect, prove, and more importantly, to prevent. Sooner or later, the American spouses tend to find out that they were duped for a Green Card by their immigrant-spouse. When that happens they often want to inform officials that they have been duped and expect that their immigrant spouses or ex-spouses will be punished and their permanent residence status in the United States will be revoked. They call, appear in person, and write letters to USCIS, Police, U.S. Department of State, Homeland Security Investigation (HSI), U.S. Immigration and Customs Enforcement (ICE), and embassies. ICE, as an agency tasked with investigating immigration fraud, has created a hotline and a website where marriage fraud can be reported. ICE has also created a Marriage Fraud Brochure (ICE, 2014b) containing basic information on immigration marriage fraud (types, penalties, and consequences), informing readers about the severity of this crime and instructing them to contact ICE by calling 1-866-DHS-2-ICE or mailing a complaint to http://www.ice.gov/about/contact.html if marriage fraud is suspected. However, according to Seminara (2008), the letters and complaints are heart-felt, but in the case of heartbreakers, even when there is clear evidence that marriages were not entered into in good faith, Green Cards are seldom invalidated. If the original petition is not approved yet, the U.S. citizen can withdraw the petition. But if the petition has been approved, the American spouse has no power to revoke the immigrant spouse's Green Card. All victims can do is to report the case.

There are more cases of "cash-for-vows" marriages than "heartbreaker marriages" (North, 2013).[1] There is no clear answer on why this is the preferred way to enter a sham marriage. While there is no one clear answer as to why "cash-for-vows" is the most popular form of entering into a sham marriage, they are fast and it is a relatively convenient business transaction for an immigrant to simply pay for an American spouse. Such an arrangement avoids all the hassles associated with having to actually find a person, making her/him fall in love, building a relationship, and deceiving the victim for at least two years while living together.

In the case of "cash-for-vows" marriage parties, both U.S. citizens and foreign spouses knowingly participate in the criminal activity and both are offenders. From the legal point of view, the involvement of U.S. citizens in this activity adds a new component, as they are involved in criminal activity that may weaken their own nation's security system. In their brochure on immigration marriage fraud, ICE reminds readers that this is a serious federal crime because participating U.S. citizens are "trading America's security for financial gain" (ICE, 2014, p. 2). They may knowingly or unknowingly be aiding terrorists, foreign intelligence, or other criminal organizations (ICE, 2014). This is not considered by authorities to be a victimless and innocent crime. It needs more attention from researchers and the public. To improve the system, it is necessary to learn about the experiences of the people involved in marriage fraud and to understand the reasons behind their decision to enter a sham marriage.

Homeland Security Investigations (HSI) is actively trying to draw attention to the problem of immigration marriage fraud. In 2013, the U.S. Immigration and Customs Enforcement's HSI Special Agent Todd Siegel started spearheading an HSI nationwide campaign to educate the public on the dangers of marriage fraud and to prevent new cases from occurring. HSI initiated more active training for ICE officers to learn how to recognize fraud, increased efforts to raise public awareness, and produced visible media and literature designed to deter individuals from getting married under false pretenses (ICE, 2014a, Top Story). The seriousness of this crime and its relation to the crimmigration nexus justify the need for research in this direction. The macro and micro issues related to immigration presented below will shed more light on the unique situation of immigrants in the United States and what factors play a role on their way to becoming criminals.

Over the last 10 years, immigration has emerged as a top issue in the United States. According to a Gallup poll conducted in July 2014, one in six Americans say immigration is the United States' most important problem (Gallup, 2014). It is hard to deny that the consequences of crimmigration increase significance of a general immigration problem—as it is affecting not only undocumented immigrants, but also legal permanent residents and U.S. citizens. Fan (2013) organizes immigration problems into three categories:

(1) investigating Americans of particular racial and ethnic backgrounds as potential aliens, (2) spending extra millions to prosecute immigrants without criminal histories before civilly deporting them, and (3) paying billions to confine immigrants who do not pose a flight or danger risk in a massively expanded civil incarceration complex. (p. 107)

As a result of America's struggle with this multidimensional problem, on November 20, 2014, President Barack Obama announced a series of executive actions to reform immigration policy. The aim of these actions was to crack down on illegal immigration at the border, prioritize deporting felons not families, and to require certain undocumented immigrants to pass a criminal background check and to pay taxes in order to stay temporarily in the United States without fear of deportation (The White House, 2014). However, as of today, President Obama's executive actions on immigration have not yet been implemented, and the negative effects of crimmigration are increasing. Fan's (2013) categories of immigration problems bring attention to negative effects that cause great harm to the U.S. population as a whole and individuals living within its borders.

According to Fan (2013), Hispanics and Asians are the two groups most targeted by immigration control law over the last century. They are also the fastest-rising voter demographic groups that highly contributed to President Obama's re-election and, emboldened by the support they provided, they expected he would support changes in the American immigration system. However, Vazquez (2015) states that "Latinos, over the years, have consistently represented over 90% of those in immigration detention, prosecuted for immigration violations, and removed as 'criminal aliens'" (p. 599). Golash-Boza (2015) seeks causes of this disparity in the heavy policing of poor neighborhoods predominated by people of color. An example of the program that made this heavy policing possible is called "Secure Communities." This immigration enforcement program was administered by U.S. ICE from 2008 to 2014. Its main goal focused on the improvement of the removal of unauthorized immigrants convicted of crime, with a priority on removing violent offenders. In July 2015, the program was replaced by Priority Enforcement Program (PEP). The basic ideas behind its operation are similar to its precursor, Secure Communities. Opponents of this program developed a website called "Uncover the Truth about PEP Comm"[2] where they argue that PEP causes permanent separation of families through deportation and threatens public safety by eroding trust between communities and the police. On January 25, 2017, Secure Communities program was restarted by the Department of Homeland Security per an executive order signed by President Donald Trump (Executive Order 13768, titled Enhancing Public Safety in the Interior of the United States). According to Golash-Boza (2015), programs like Secure Communities do not make communities more secure. Rather they create instability and insecurity. To support this statement she references Garcia and Keyes's (2012) report that documents the everyday lives of undocumented immigrants in the first community in California that signed up to Secure Communities (North County, San Diego). The report is based on 30 in-depth interviews with migrants and 851 surveys. Garcia and Keyes (2012) found that undocumented migrants were reluctant to report crimes out of fear they could be arrested and deported. In many cases, immigrants were afraid of deportation to the extent that they avoided public places. Some parents stopped picking their children up from school. Fear and insecurity characterized the lives of many immigrants.

Moreover, those programs and policies do not target dangerous criminals. Golash-Boza (2015) pointed out that "immigration policy enforcement targets Afro-Caribbean small-time drug peddlers and Latino undocumented workers—not hardcore criminals or terrorists" (p. 8). Based on the ICE data provided to journalist Alan Gomez, in 2013, there were 133,551 interior removals and 180,970 border removals. During the same year, almost 59 percent of all removals were based on criminal convictions for one of the three crime categories: dangerous drugs, criminal traffic offenses, and immigration violations (TRAC Immigration, 2014). Some of these convictions would only be considered criminal in a very broad definition of the term. Those deported for illegal entry were converted into criminals for reporting purposes. Operation Streamline also contributes to the crimmigration effect. Started in 2005, it is a joint initiative of the Department of Homeland Security and the Department of Justice in the United States that adopts a "zero-tolerance" approach to unauthorized border crossing. It was created with the goal of combating drug trafficking, weapons trafficking, human smuggling, and repeat illegal immigration into the United States (Lydgate, 2010).

Operation Streamline has fundamentally transformed U.S. border enforcement practices. When immigrants are processed through Operation Streamline, they are getting a formal deportation, which is very different from a voluntary return. They are also charged with unauthorized entry, which is a misdemeanor. In comparison before the initiative began, when migrants were apprehended by DHS's Border Patrol agents for first-time improper entry to the United States, DHS either voluntarily returned those migrants to their home country or administratively detained them and processed them through the civil immigration system. Prosecutions were rare for first-time border crossers who lacked criminal history. Now, based on Operation Streamline, all apprehended migrants (including those apprehended for the first time) are prosecuted for misdemeanor "improper entry by alien" under 8 U.S.C. §1325, which carries a maximum sentence of six months. Any migrant who has been deported in the past and attempts to reenter can be charged with felony reentry under 8 U.S.C. §1326, which generally carries a two-year maximum penalty. However, those who try to reenter again and already have a felony on their history (for reentry or any other crime), based on the same article can be punished by up to 20 years of imprisonment (Lydgate, 2010). Very systematic criminalization efforts along the southern border cannot be denied. This is a direct result of the "zero-tolerance"' policies to a border crossing.

Most of America's immigrants (those apprehended while attempting to cross the border and unauthorized immigrants who are already in the United States) have no prior criminal convictions. They have usually attempted to cross the border in search of work or to reunite with family in the United States. Enhanced deportation tactics increasingly deport people with strong ties to the United States. As Golash-Boza (2015) explains, "Instead of making us safe, mass deportations tear families apart and prevent immigrants from applying for legalization or citizenship even when they qualify" (p. 10).

Moreover, initiatives like Operation Streamline are likely to keep undocumented immigrants in the United States. This phenomenon is called "reduced circularity in migration"—severe punishments for unauthorized border crossing and high risk of apprehension prevent undocumented immigrants from leaving once they have arrived (Lydgate, 2010). Those who were unsuccessful and apprehended end up in detention facilities, seated side by side in a cell with drug dealers, smugglers, and other criminals. They are being introduced to alternative means and structures from different networks to which they otherwise would never have been exposed.

Another cause for concern that emerges out of new immigration policies is the cost of crimmigration. Fan (2013) states that American taxpayers pay billions to confine nondangerous immigrants in a massively expanded civil incarceration complex. Lydgate (2010) analyzes the cost of Operation Streamline that has drastically increased immigration prosecutions while requiring increased funding for DHS to support the Border Patrol agents, agency attorneys, significant funding for the district courts, U.S. Attorney's offices, federal public defenders, CJA Panel attorneys, court interpreters, U.S. Marshals, Office of the Federal Detention Trustee, and detention centers in each of the federal districts along the border. The costs are likely significant. Burridge (2009) estimates that it costs around $9 to $11 million a month to detain those incarcerated under Operation Streamline.[3] Additionally, it costs approximately $10,000 a day to provide defense attorneys for immigrants. Furthermore, it costs $88 a day to house a prisoner in privately run facilities, and $120 a day at ICE processing centers.

As the world's largest recipient of immigrants (World Bank, 2011), the United States has to deal with many complex problems linked to immigration. Those who support immigration usually highlight its contribution to economic growth (Hanson, 2012); opponents mostly point to reduced economic opportunities for U.S. citizens who are forced to compete with immigrants for limited resources. Regardless of which position one takes (for or against immigration), it is certain that immigrants influence the economic situation in the country. This is why accurate statistics on all immigrants (documented as well as undocumented) are essential to assessing the social, economic, and demographic future of the United States. However, immigration statistics are the weakest link in the demographic accounting system (Massey, 2010). There are ongoing debates, particularly at the national political level; however, during those debates an important voice is often missing from the overall conversation—that of the immigration community itself (Talwar, et al., 2012). Illegal immigrants represent a hidden population. No research to date has examined this population; therefore, no sampling frame exists. Those who participate in sham marriages are hardly accessible because public acknowledgment of membership in this population is potentially threatening. Moreover, this population is difficult to access "because standard probability methods produce low response rates and responses that lack candor" (Hecka-thorn, 1997, p. 174). However, it is important to find a way to access this population to understand the dynamics of GCMF.

The United States is a home for 11.96 million unauthorized immigrants (Baker, 2018). This is too large a number to be simply omitted from con-sideration. Moreover, sham marriages affect the lives of those involved in it (immigrants themselves, U.S. citizens, and their families) as well as those not involved. There is no clear estimate on how many sham marriages take place because no official data on this issue currently exist. One way to approach the topic is to read and analyze fraud marriage-related press stories or interview INS officials or USCIS officers (see North, 2013; Seminara, 2008). Very general estimates can be derived from publicly accessible USCIS data that contains information on alien relative petitions. The available online docu-ments indicate the number of petitions received, approved, denied, and pend-ing. These are displayed by the quarter of each fiscal year for every federal agency office. Based on this data, in 2018, USCIS received 583,020 Green Card petitions to sponsor "Immediate Relatives of U.S. citizens":[4] 520,498 were approved, and 40,492 denied (USCIS, 2018). However, the "Immediate Relatives" category includes spouses, children, and parents of U.S. citizens. There is no data available where the number of approved or denied petitions for spouses is separated from the number of parents and children of U.S. citi-zens. In other words, the number of approved and denied petitions is an ag-gregate of all three groups of relatives of U.S. citizens: spouses, parents, and children. But the U.S. Department of Homeland Security data (2018, Table 7) show that 54 percent of all petitions for "Immediate Relatives of U.S. citizen" are submitted for spouses, 16 percent for children, and 30 percent for parents. Based on the online search of press stories, reports, and articles there was no information available on cases where someone was trying to fraudulently obtain a Green Card based on "Immediate Relatives of U.S. citizens" from a parent or child of a U.S. citizen. In contrast, there is plenty of information available on fraud marriage cases. It does not mean that cases involving par-ents or children do not take place, but certainly, they occur at a much lower rate than spousal-cases. Therefore, most of denied petitions presumably are connected with Green Card marriage fraud. ICE (2014b) highlights that this activity is perceived as a "threat to U.S. national security, financial institu-tions and the integrity of the immigration system" (p. 2).

Every year, approximately one million Green Cards are issued in the United States. In 2018, 1,096,611 were issued (DHS, 2018, Table 1). Almost 25 percent of Green Cards (exactly 268,149) were obtained by aliens based on their marriage with a U.S. citizen (DHS, 2018, Table 7). No doubt, some of them were fraudulent—that is, entered into for the sole purpose of getting the immigrant a Green Card. According to the House Report on Immigration Marriage Fraud Amendments of 1986 (IMFA), "[s]urveys conducted by the Immigration and Naturalization Service have revealed that approximately thirty percent of all petitions for immigrant visas involve suspect marital relationships." The most current USCIS data shows that in 2018, approximately 6.9 percent (USCIS, 2018) of I-130 (Petition for Alien Relative) petitions for Immediate Relatives of U.S. citizens were denied.

Despite these statistics, marriage fraud for the purpose of immigration benefits gets very little notice or debate in the public arena, and the State Department and Department of Homeland Security has nowhere near the resources needed to combat the problem (Seminara, 2008). There have been just a few in-depth examinations of this topic (Seminara, 2008). From the legal point of view, marriage fraud can be seen as posing a significant threat to the integrity of the immigration system but also to national security (ICE, 2014a). The U.S. ICE has raised concerns of possible terrorism risks. If some uneducated aliens without financial resources are able to defraud the system and obtain Green Cards with so little resistance, then surely terrorists can do so as well (Seminara, 2008). ICE warns U.S. citizens that terrorists can "hide their identity, gain unlawful employment, access government buildings, and open bank accounts and businesses to conduct further criminal activity" (ICE, 2014b, p. 2) and if they participate in marriage fraud, they may be held accountable for aiding terrorists, foreign intelligence, or other criminal organizations.

Although immigration marriage fraud is a serious federal offense, those who participate in it should be viewed not only through the lens of their criminal activity but also through their experiences that led them to be involved in it. The understanding of life experiences pre and post arrival in the United States will help to understand reasons why foreigners decide to pay American citizens for Green Cards.

NOTES

1. Based on reading the immigration-related press stories collected daily by the eagled-eyed staff of CIS and private conversation with ex-INS officials.

2. See http://www.truthaboutpep.com/.

3. Based on information from *Coalicón de Derechos Humanos*–a grassroots immigrant rights project in Tucson, Arizona.

4. Some applications approved, denied, or pending a decision may have been received in prior reporting periods.

Chapter Four

Criminological Aspects
of Marriage Fraud

The grounded theory approach relies on a specific research methodology that was developed in the 1960s by two sociologists: Barney Glaser and Anselm Strauss (Willig, 2013). Glaser and Strauss (1967) put "a high emphasis on theory as a process; that is theory as an ever-developing entity, not as a perfected product" (p. 32). The grounded theory method of research seeks to develop new theories based on the data collected. Instead of attempting to apply previous models and theories onto new data, the grounded theory approach, through a series of steps, provides a theory that is actually being derived from the current data set (Strauss and Corbin, 1998). Such theories are therefore "grounded" in the data from which they have emerged, rather than relying on analytical constructs, categories, or variables from pre-existing theories. Grounded theory is "designed to open up a space for the development of new, contextualized theories" (Willig, 2013, p. 69). They are particularly useful for developing new and context-based theories in the social sciences.

When the novelty of a studied topic causes a lack of clear directions on what aspects should be mainly explored, standardized tools such as surveys are of little use. The qualitative approach aims to understand the social world from the viewpoint of respondents, through detailed descriptions of their actions (by understanding who they really are through their actions), and through the richness of meaning associated with observable behavior (Wildemuth, 1993).

A distinguishing advantage of the grounded theory approach is the opportunity for the emergence of new theories. This also makes it a valuable method when contemporary theories are inadequate or fail to exist altogether (Creswell, 2009). The grounded theory design becomes a routine based, qualitative process that is intended to develop a theory to explain a process, action, or interaction on a broad conceptual level (Creswell, 2009), for example, how certain criminal activities develop among specific groups. In this case, grounded theory may help explain how Green Card marriage fraud (GCMF) develops among immigrant populations.

The current research has relied on the participants' views of GCMF and the circumstances relating to this phenomenon. The importance of culture is addressed in the study as well as the circumstances of the participants. A social constructionist approach to grounded theory allows the researcher to look for the cause of observed reality while preserving the complexity of social life. Grounded theory is a method that researchers apply through inquiry and provides them a chance to understand research participants' social constructions (Charmaz, 2002). The use of social constructionist approach not only provides the opportunity to explore the GCMF phenomenon but also to partially explain why it occurs from the perspective of those involved in it.

Existing theoretical perspectives can help to frame and perhaps explain some of the dynamics within immigrant populations on their way to permanent residency. Cornish and Clarke's (1987) rational choice theory, as well as Stumpf's (2006) membership theory and the crimmigration concept are utilized in order to help frame and ultimately understand rationalizations and the choices made by immigrants on their way to U.S. citizenship. Rational choice theory has been successfully used in a large number of studies explaining why criminals decided to engage in illegal activity (see Benson, 1985; Bentham, 1823; Entorf, 2000; Scully and Marolla, 1984; Vieraitis et al., 2012).

GCMF is an understudied crime. Yet, immigrants constitute a unique group and any decision made to engage in GCMF has important consequences for society at large. For the purpose of completing this study, individual interviews were conducted and the participants' situation was examined through the lens of Stumpf's (2006) membership theory and the "crimmigration" concept.

This study was also placed in the context of rational choice theory (Cornish and Clarke, 1987). This theory draws on classic theory and economic theories of crime, and states "crimes are broadly the result of rational choices based on analyses of anticipated cost and benefits" (Cornish and Clarke, 1986, p. vi). Individuals choose to engage in crime in an effort to maximize their benefits and minimize their costs. The benefits of crime can be tangible (money or property) or intangible (e.g., respect of peers, retribution, and sense of accomplishment). Costs of crime may include formal punishment (e.g., arrest, prison time, fine) or informal (e.g., guilt, anxiety, fear, shame, social stigma). A prospective offender considers multiple costs and benefits prior to making a decision about committing a crime.

Rational choice theory (Cornish and Clarke, 1987) has helped to frame this research. The process occurs in two major stages. The first stage is called the "initial involvement model" where individuals decide whether they are willing to become involved in crime to satisfy their needs. The second stage is called the "criminal event model" where individuals make a decision about engaging in crime and must decide to commit a particular offense. This decision is heavily influenced by the immediate situation of the potential offender (Cornish and Clarke, 1986). Cornish and Clarke (1986) argue that separate theoretical models are necessary for particular types of crime. Hence, the decision process leading to burglary is different from the decision process for illegal immigration.

Rational choice theory can make an important contribution to understanding the purpose of immigration and GCMF. In this context, the theory borrows from neoclassical microeconomics. Migration is viewed as a rational action, maximizing the individual's net benefits (Todaro, 1976). According to Haug (2008), human capital is a determining factor in migration decisions, and this decision-making process correlates with the probability of finding a job and with the wage level at the place of destination. Haug (2008) continues by elaborating on households' economy; distribution of incomes and benefits within households seems to have a greater impact on the decision to migrate than individual income level. Both monetary and non-monetary costs and benefits can play a role (Sjaastad, 1962). In that sense, migration is in essence a family strategy. When choosing the best place for the family, one rationalizes the decision by maximizing the sum of utilities over several dimensions like wealth, status, comfort, suggestion, autonomy, affiliation, and morality (De Jong and Fawcett, 1981). Location-specific capital (social relationships) at the place of destination also influences decisions about migration (Haug, 2008). However, every case is unique. There is no list of necessary and adequate push or pull factors. Moreover, weighting of different utility factors is challenging (especially when comparing monetary and nonmonetary factors). From this perspective, every potential immigrant weighs the potential gains and losses that may come with migration and bases the favorable side of this equation. Using this approach, immigrants are like anyone else, behaving as rational utility maximizers, responding to economic incentives.

However, the decision regarding migration is not the only rational choice that one makes. Once immigrants have arrived at their destination, their rational decision-making process must continue in order to fulfill the plan created before migration. Immigrants are faced with immediate concerns that are almost exclusively practical in nature and require a series of essentially self-interested decisions. A Green Card may be a remedy for many concerns.

Therefore, immigrants weigh costs and benefits of GCMF by deciding whether or not achieving permanent residency status will maximize their benefits. The benefits may include access to better job opportunities, college education, health insurance, sense of belonging, and other considerations. Costs include primarily risk of imprisonment, fine, and deportation.

The rational choice explanation for the illegal behavior of undocumented immigrants has also been explored by Entorf (2000). He focuses on three basic elements: (a) the income differential between the receiving and the sending countries, (b) the severity of sanctions, and (c) the probability of being detected.

> This situation fits the point of departure of the more general theory of illegal behavior, in which the considered income differential would be the difference between low legal income opportunities in the home country, and high and risky illegal income opportunities in the host country. (Entorf, 2000, p. 10)

Using Bentham (1788) and Becker's (1968) approaches Entorf (2000) concludes that illegal immigrants are just like anyone else.[1] They behave as rational utility maximizers and respond to economic incentives. Although Entorf (2000) does not refer to Green Card marriages, he shows how undocumented immigrants make their rational choices considering income differentials (difference between low legal income opportunities in the home country, and high and risky illegal income opportunities in the host country) acting as an incentive strong enough to overcome risks that come with life without a legal status.

Taking Entorf's (2000) study as a model, rational choice theory helps contextualize the behaviors of all three groups interviewed in this study: immigrants and U.S. citizens participating in the GCMF, and marriage fraud brokers. Immigrants and U.S. citizens treat the Green Card as a business transaction. Chi and Drewianka (2014) tried to estimate "How much is a Green Card worth?" for immigrants. They found that immigrants whose wages have been most affected by their inability to seek alternative employment (usually due to the lack of the required work permit) had the strongest incentive to seek a U.S. citizen-spouse to help them obtain permanent residency status. For many immigrants, GCMF is an investment. When engaging in a "cash-for-vows" marriage, they invest their money hoping to get a return on their investment. They weigh the benefits versus the risks involved. Aware of all the benefits that come with permanent residency, they make a rational choice in regard to their involvement in an attempt to maximize their benefits. U.S. citizens also weigh benefits versus risks. Unlike immigrants who get multiple benefits from this type of fraud, U.S. citizens just receive financial gain. They enter the transaction motivated by money and by the possibility of making a profit. Presented in Chapter 9, Acquah's case shows that the same rationale can be applied to marriage fraud brokers. Their only benefit from arranging such marriages is financial gain, having weighed the risk of being caught against the money they can make.

GCMFs are undoubtedly a contributing factor to increased calls for the prosecution of undocumented immigrants. The term "crimmigration law" is relatively new. It was developed by Juliet Stumpf (2006) and reflects the intersection of criminal law and immigration law, or in other words, criminalization of immigration law. She applies membership theory to map the exclusionary effects of the crimmigration. Based on this theory, individual rights and privileges are limited to the members of a social contract between the government and the people. Some individuals are included in the social contract, while others are excluded. American society is divided into two groups: members and nonmembers. The latter create a class of outsiders without access to many rights and privileges that come with membership. The state decides who is permitted to live in the United States and become a member of the American population and who is to be expelled from this society.

The group of nonmembers steadily increases, while the number of members decreases (as the number of undocumented immigrants in the United States is growing). As a result, society is becoming "increasingly stratified by flexible conceptions of membership in which nonmembers are cast out of the community by means of borders, walls, rules, and public condemnation" (Stumpf, 2006, p. 419). This system of exclusion conflicts with the need to integrate noncitizens into society and may result in alienation and contribute to the commission of further crimes (Stumpf, 2006). The costs become greater when attention is given to socioeconomic characteristics of excluded populations. Latinos are deported from the United States at extremely higher rates than non-Latino immigrants. Vazquez (2015) estimates that over the years they have consistently represented over 90 percent of those in immigration detention, prosecuted for immigration violations, and regarded as criminal aliens. They are seen as a danger to national security and public safety. Stumpf (2006) adds that immigration law tends to exclude people of color (in general) and people with lower socioeconomic status. This tendency is also visible when examining entry to the country instead of removals. Noncitizens with low socioeconomic status have lower chances for obtaining visas and longer waiting periods for decisions in their cases. On the other hand, the entry of certain professionals, managers, executives, and investors are given priority. The number of deportees is rapidly increasing. The United States does not have enough facilities for the detainment of noncitizens. According to Ortega and Lacsh (2014, p. 257), "This opened opportunities for the private prison industry to accommodate the demand for more for-profit facilities."

Since immigrants constitute a significant proportion of the population in the United States, society needs to know as much as possible about the quality of their lives and challenges they are facing. The crimmigration phenomenon is quickly gaining widespread recognition with many new challenges. It is desirable to know the reasons why persons decide to leave their homeland, their experience of migration, their resources to function in unfamiliar environments, and the receptiveness of the new host country to their presence (Segal and Mayadas, 2005). It is also beneficial to know how the laws impact them, why they decide to break the law, and if they are at a higher risk of breaking the law again. If we understand their experiences, we may understand the reasons why they engage in GCMF and the impact which immigration and criminal laws are having on their lives. Knowledge about the causes of their decisions and choices in relation to immigration fraud may help in the development of successful methods to prevent such fraud. This knowledge can be acquired only based on in-depth studies. Edmonston (1996) argues that new studies need to distinguish among illegal aliens, legal immigrants, and refugees. Furthermore, such research is needed to learn more about the culture of immigrant groups and the legal processes involved. For many immigrants, achieving legal status in a new country may have enormous consequences for both the concerned immigrants and their new countries.

NOTE

1. Each individual is motivated solely by the desire to maximize the magnitude of his or her "happiness" and minimize the magnitude of "pain."

Part II

A CASE STUDY: "CASH-FOR-VOWS"

Chapter Five

The Research Design

There has been limited research on paths to U.S. citizenship for foreign-born persons from the perspective of those involved in the process. This is especially true with respect to research focusing on Green Card marriage fraud involving a "cash-for-vows" scam. This study fills in this gap in criminological understanding and theory by exploring the experiences of people who have actually admitted participating in such schemes.

This research is designed to understand the motivations of Green Card marriage fraud participants by detailing their experiences as they undertake the bureaucratic steps required for obtaining the status of permanent residency. Various factors which may be responsible for attracting immigrants to this criminal activity are identified. A grounded theory approach was used to develop a general explanation of the fraudulent acts revealed by a group of selected participants (see: Creswell et al. 2007; Fassinger 2005).[1]

The research participants were immigrants, U.S. citizens who participated in Green Card marriage fraud, and marriage fraud brokers. These informants provided valuable first-hand accounts of the social, individual, and legal factors associated with their participation in this type of federal crime. Due to lack of legal status in this country, unauthorized immigrants are members of a "hidden population" which makes them inaccessible, and this has implications for the development of a sampling frame from which one would derive population estimates. Marriage fraud brokers are also a "hidden population" because their involvement in an illegal activity makes them less likely to cooperate with researchers. There is no known pool of such marriage fraud brokers to access in prison or in other programs commonly utilized in criminological research, also making them inaccessible and precludes the development of a sampling frame required for deriving population estimates. Therefore, traditional survey methods are impractical for these populations.

In order to overcome these obstacles and to learn more about these hidden groups, face-to-face in-person interviews were utilized for data collection.

Cornish and Clarke's (1987) rational choice theory and membership theory, the crimmigration concept by Stumpf (2006) as well as Sykes and Matza's (1957) neutralization theory served as theoretical frames for the qualitative research aspects of this book.

The "cash-for-vows" scheme is a very common type of marriage fraud and more easily identified by federal law enforcement. As soon as the fact of paying for the service is proven, the marriage is considered fraud. What is more important for criminological research, this act is criminal in all respects: people are paying to get illegal access to benefits to which they are not entitled to. In the case of other types of marriage fraud that do not involve "cash-for-vows," more complicating issues are involved. One case in point is when two people are trying to make a life together and this is sometimes considered good enough to classify as legitimate marriage.

The informants shared their knowledge through qualitative interviews and were recruited by using the "snowball sampling method."[2] For a pre-test, several persons who had participated in marriage fraud were interviewed. The pre-test was designed to determine the likely success of recruiting participants into the study. This pilot study was also designed to elicit information on the crime and the motivations and rationale for committing these acts in accordance with provisions that would protect the participants' confidentiality and protect them from potential harms. Pre-testing suggested the selected theoretical framework was suitable for the purpose of this study and encouraged further use of the selected methods and procedures of data collection.

The initial research process started with three cultural guides (informants) known to the researcher. These three informants were from different countries and cultural groups because it was expected that immigrants from different countries developed unique patterns of dealing with Green Card marriages. Cultural guides were asked to share an invitation to participate in this research with potential participants (Green Card marriage fraud participants and brokers). At the time of each initial interview, participants were told that they may refer to the researcher or other individuals they knew who had been through similar circumstances. The same approach was used during the main study for finding study participants.

The interviews conducted in the study were held at times and locations convenient for participants; however, chosen places were public such as restaurants, cafeterias, or parks (to assure the safety of participants and the interviewer). Each location also had to provide an opportunity for a comfortable private conversation; consequently, night hours (10 p.m.–6 a.m.) were excluded. When a participant met the researcher, a consent form was reviewed with the participant and signed. At the end of the interview, participants were asked to tell others with experiences similar to theirs (i.e., engaged in Green Card marriage fraud as either immigrants or U.S. citizens) about an opportunity to participate in the research. Similarly, marriage fraud brokers were also asked to refer other marriage fraud brokers. Such brokers were considered key informants since they were most likely to have a disproportionate weight and role in the conduct and outcome of the research in this study.

In total (pre-test and main phase), 30 interviews were successfully conducted: 17 with U.S. citizens, 10 with immigrants, and 3 with marriage fraud brokers. The interviews took place during the period from 2015–2016.[3] All participants were residents of Massachusetts. With their permission, all interviews were audio recorded, transcribed by the researcher, and analyzed. All participants received incentives in a form of gift cards to convenient stores (Walgreens, CVS) and/or fast food restaurants (McDonald, Dunkin Donuts). The incentive amount was set up on the level that compensates interviewees for their time.

Questions were open-ended and presented during one-on-one, in-person interviews with adults who participated in marriage fraud for immigration purposes. All participants were asked about their understanding and meaning of engaging in Green Card marriage fraud and their perceived level of responsibility for the acts they committed that constituted a crime in the United States Demographic characteristics, socioeconomic, and other related background information were collected, but no identifying information was included. All participants were informed of the right to terminate the interview at any time. Two participants decided to discontinue an interview stating that they did not want to answer these types of questions. NVivo, a qualitative data analysis software package, was used to assist with the author's memo writing and coding.[4]

NOTES

1. The strategy of inquiry undertaken in this study is a qualitative grounded theory approach based on a social constructivist approach. This interpretive framework accepts that reality is a product of the human mind interacting with experience in the real world. Individuals seek to understand their world and develop their own particular, subjective meanings that correspond to their experience (Creswell, 2009). Social constructivists view knowledge as created by the interactions of individuals within a society (Andrews, 2012). Hence, this research was designed to rely on the participants' views of the situation being studied. When studying hidden populations like immigrants engaging in Green Card marriage fraud, a social constructivist approach permitted a full exploration of dynamics within the sampled population. For

a researcher the goal is to discover the world as it is experienced by those involved in Green Card marriage fraud, to understand the nature of participants' experience and the meaning that they attach to their experiences. As such, the study's design used open-ended questions to stimulate participants to share their views the way they want to share. Such a grounded theory approach provides the opportunity to collect new information and consider, refine, and develop new theories. Thus, this grounded theory approach necessitated deciding not only what data to collect next, but where to find it in order to develop any emerging theories.

2. A "snowball" sampling technique was used to recruit participants for this study. It is a nonprobability sampling technique. As Biernacki and Waldorf (1981) highlighted, chain referrals are well suited for studies focusing on sensitive issues, concerning private matter, and thus requiring the knowledge of insiders to locate potential study participants. Green Card marriage frauds are definitely sensitive and private issues; hence, the selection of this nonprobability sampling technique.

3. Morse (1994) recommends for grounded theory methodology that the research should start with 30–50 interviews, while Creswell (1998) suggests only 20–30. A number between those two measures, 30, is most often used in qualitative research. For example, Garcia and Keyes (2012) conducted 30 in-depth interviews with immigrants on the topic of restrictions in the U.S. receiving communities and that number was sufficient to obtain satisfying and rich data. In the current study, the total targeted sample size was 36. Targeted sample size for the first group (immigrants and U.S. citizens who participated in Green Card marriage) was 30. The researcher had planned to include six marriage fraud brokers.

4. The author's thoughts and observations were recorded as memos. Memos related to a particular project aspect or interviews were linked together. Codes or nodes were created as they were generated from the data. There was no pre-existing theory used to develop codes (or nodes in NVivo parlance). NVivo helped with targeting key words, and organizing and mapping most frequently used words and patterns of answers.

Chapter Six

Defining Key Terms and Protection of Subjects

In order to better understand the experiences of individuals involved in Green Card marriage frauds and their reasons for such participation, this chapter briefly describes and defines several key terms. These include: Green Card; Green Card marriage fraud; "cash-for-vows"; Green Card marriage participant; and marriage fraud broker. In addition, due to the sensitive nature of the topic, this chapter reviews several of the steps which were taken to protect the identity of subjects and their information. For example, the audio recording of a participant's interview was stored on a locked password protected hard drive immediately following each interview and all folders were password protected. Furthermore, no identifying information was included in research interview data or files.

A "Green Card" is a common name for Permanent Resident Cards (Form I-551) issued by the United States Citizenship and Immigration Services to non-U.S. citizen individuals granted authorization to live and work in the United States on a permanent basis. Non-U.S. citizens who are residing in the United States under legally recognized and lawfully recorded permanent residence as immigrants are called "Green Card Holders" or "Permanent Resident Aliens."

"Green Card marriage fraud" (also called sham or fraudulent marriage) is a marriage between a non-U.S. citizen and a U.S. citizen, entered into for the sole purpose of obtaining a lawful permanent resident status in the United States by a non-U.S. citizen (exemplified by receipt of the Green Card).

A "cash-for-vows" Green Card marriage is a marriage entered into for the sole purpose of obtaining a Green Card and involves an immigrant paying a U.S. citizen to marry. Both spouses are aware of the business nature of their marriage and they knowingly agree to participate in it. Payment methods and form vary. It could be either a one-time payment or installment payments spread over the duration of the marriage. Forms may include, but are not limited to, cash, electronic transfer, valuable items (like phone or car), payments for living expenses of U.S. citizen (like rent and bills), payment for college expenses, or a mix of these forms. In the section of the book concerned with research findings, the words "cash-for-vows Green Card marriage fraud" is condensed and more simply identified as "Green Card marriage fraud."

Participants of Green Card marriage fraud in this study include two groups: immigrants (non-U.S. citizens) and U.S. citizens. Immigrants/non-U.S. citizens are defined as foreign-born individuals who are in the United States in order to settle or reside. In this research, the intent to settle is conjectural, based on the attempt to obtain the permanent resident status (through Green Card marriage fraud). Immigrants may have legal or no legal status. Legal status means that the immigrant has a valid visa or other legal and valid permission to stay in the United States for a specified period of time; while without legal status (called "illegal" status) means that the immigrant lacks a legal right to be in the United States, having either entered the country without inspection or having stayed beyond the expiration date of a visa or other status. Both immigrants with legal and no legal status were eligible to become participants in this study and are referred to simply as "immigrants." In order to take part in this study, the participating immigrants must have confirmed that they entered into marriage with U.S. citizens solely for the purpose of obtaining a Green Card. Moreover, participation was limited to those who confirmed that following the marriage they had already taken at least a first step in the process of obtaining a Green Card, that is, their spouse submitted Form I-130 (Petition for Alien Relative) to the USCIS.

The term "U.S. citizen" in this study refers to an individual with status as a U.S. citizen because of: being born in the United States, having a U.S. citizen parent,[1] or being a former alien who has been naturalized as a U.S. citizen (as defined by 8 U.S. Code § 1401). U.S. citizen participants in this research had to confirm that they married an immigrant to allow him/her to obtain a Green Card (as an immediate relative of a U.S. citizen) in exchange for financial gain. Additionally, participation was limited to those who stated that they had already taken at least a first step in the process to obtain permanent residency for their immigrant spouse, by submitting Form I-130 (Petition for Alien Relative) to the USCIS.

A "marriage fraud broker" is a person who arranges Green Card marriages (for the purpose of this study those interviewed had to have arranged a minimum of three such marriages) between an immigrant and a U.S. citizen in exchange for financial gain.

A number of steps were undertaken to ensure that interviewees would not experience any adverse effects. In general, the risks that the author/researcher guarded against were: (1) psychological strain resulting from intrusive questions concerning personal matters of a sensitive nature; and (2) the disclosure of confidential information to others. In order to contend with any possible emotional distress, interviewees were informed that they could terminate or interrupt the interview and all interviewees were provided with a "resources factsheet" listing agencies offering relevant assistance.

As previously indicated interviews took place in locations that did not arouse suspicion and that provided privacy for the conversation. The preferences of potential participants and safety of all parties in regard to such locations were taken into consideration.

In order to reduce the risk of participant identification, marriage fraud brokers who were asked to refer potential participants were asked to simply tell them how to contact the researcher's office if they were interested in being interviewed. Contact information of these potential participants was not stored. Additionally, the marriage fraud brokers were not informed about who decided to participate and who did not.

Audio recordings of participant interviews were transferred to a password-protected hard drive immediately following an interview. The audio recorder was cleared of all data after data transfer. All folders were password protected. Careful monitoring of the data storage was maintained. In order to protect disclosure of confidential information, the audio recordings of interviews did not include any identifying information other than demographic information (race, ethnicity, age, and gender). The participants were given an alias name to use during the interview and were advised also to use alias names when they spoke of other people to prevent identification of themselves or others. Whenever identifying information was inadvertently conveyed during the interview, it was deleted and not included in the transcription.

NOTE

1. The Child Citizenship Act of 2000 provides automatic acquisition of U.S. citizenship when certain conditions have been met.

Part III

INSIDE THE GREEN CARD MARRIAGE FRAUD PHENOMENON

Chapter Seven

Demographics and Other Parameters

In total (pre-test and main phase), 58 individuals who participated in Green Card marriage fraud (GCMF) were targeted. Thirty interviews were successfully conducted: 17 with U.S. citizens, 10 with immigrants, and 3 with marriage fraud brokers. Table 1 contains characteristics of those who participated in the interview and Table 2 presents characteristics of those who refused.

As presented in Tables 7.1 and 7.2, between 58 individuals who participated in GCMF, 29 are females and 29 are males. Racial distribution is as follows: 21 Caucasians, 32 African Americans, and 5 individuals who classify themselves as two or more races.[1] Moreover, eight GCMF participants identified themselves as being of Hispanic origins. Their ages spanned from 22 to 55 years, and mean age is 30 years and four months. However, most of the participants (52 percent) are between the age of 22 and 29.

The age of study participants and potential participants[2] is presented below in Figures 7.1 and 7.2 (respectively).

Thirty-one immigrants who participated in GCMF were approached for interviews. Of these, 10 agreed to be interviewed (32 percent). The group was diverse based on their nationality: three participants were from Ghana, and one each from Poland, Colombia, Ukraine, Nigeria, Haiti, Trinidad, and Russia. Those who refused to participate in the interview additionally included individuals from Dominican Republic, Jamaica, Kenya, and Serbia.

The age of participating immigrants spanned from 23 to 38 years, with a mean age of 30 years and seven months. Six participants (60 percent) were in their twenties (to be exact between 23 and 29 years old). Within this group were eight males and two females. Four participants were Caucasian and six were African Americans. Only one between them identified as Hispanic.

Table 7.1. Description of the Interviewees

Interviewed GCMF Participants

Name	Sex	Race	Hispanic	Education	Employment	Monthly Income	Country of Origin
Jan	M	Caucasian	No	MA	FT & PT (2nd job)	$4,000 & $1,000	Poland
Miguel	M	Caucasian	Yes	Some college	FT	$1,300	Columbia
Vladimir	M	Caucasian	No	Some college	FT	$1,600	Ukraine
Kofi	M	African American	No	Some college	PT	$1,600	Ghana
Steven*	M	African American	No	MA	FT	$2,500	Nigeria
Bruce	M	African American	No	BA	FT	$4,000	Ghana
Francis	M	African American	No	MA	Unemployed	$0	Ghana
Natalie	F	African American	No	BA	PT	$700	Haiti
Frank	M	African American	No	12th grade	FT	$5,000	Trinidad
Tania	F	Caucasian	No	BA	FT	$3,000	Russia
Elizabeth*	F	African American	No	Some college	FT	$1,000	USA
Anna	F	Caucasian	No	MA	Unemployed	$0	USA
Paula	F	Caucasian	Yes	MA	FT	$2,000	USA

Name	Sex	Race		Education	Employment	Income	Country
Naomi*	F	African American	No	Some college	PT	$972	USA
Lori	F	African American	No	HS	Unemployed	$0	USA
Yolanda	F	African American	No	HS	PT	$1,000	USA
Juana	F	Caucasian	Yes	Some college	FT	$1,600	USA
Rob	M	African American	No	GED	Temp.	$1,050	USA
Jamal	M	African American	No	Some college	FT	$2,500	USA
Ashley	F	Caucasian	Yes	Some college	Unemployed	$0	USA
Trice	F	African American	No	12th grade	FT	$1,500	USA
Shelly	F	African American	No	Some college	FT	$900	USA
Gloria	F	African American	No	Some college	FT	$1,000	USA
Amy	F	Two races	No	HS	FT	$1,500	USA
David	M	Two races	No	Some college	Unemployed	$0	USA
Daniel	M	African American	No	Some college	FT	$1,500	USA
Joe	M	Two races	No	BS	FT	$2,500	USA
Anita	F	African American	No	Some college	Unemployed	$0	USA

*CGCMF brokers. Two out of three marriage fraud brokers got married themselves in order to evade the immigration laws. Therefore, the number of participants is 28 because two brokers were interviewed as marriage brokers and as GCMF participants.

Legend: M–Male, F–Female, FT–Full time, PT–Part time, Temp–Temporary work, HS–High School, BA–Bachelor of Arts, BS–Bachelor of Science, MA–Master of Arts.

Table 7.2.   Description of the Individuals Who Engaged in the GCMF but Refused to Participate in the Interview

Sex	Race	Hispanic	Country of Origin
M	Caucasian	No	Serbia
M	African American	No	Ghana
M	African American	No	Nigeria
M	Caucasian	No	Ukraine
M	Caucasian	No	Turkey
M	Caucasian	No	Turkey
M	African American	No	Ghana
F	African American	No	Nigeria
F	African American	No	Kenya
M	Two races	Yes	Dominican Republic
M	Caucasian	No	Poland
M	African American	No	Ghana
F	Caucasian	No	Russia
F	Caucasian	No	Russia
F	Caucasian	No	Russia
F	Caucasian	No	Romania
M	Caucasian	No	Poland
M	African American	No	Jamaica
M	African American	No	Haiti
M	African American	No	Haiti
F	African American	No	Kenya
F	African American	No	USA
F	African American	No	USA
F	Caucasian	Yes	USA
F	Caucasian	Yes	USA
F	African American	No	USA
M	Two races	No	USA
F	African American	No	USA
F	Caucasian	No	USA
M	African American	Yes	USA

Seven immigrants had full-time employment, two had part-time employment, and one person was unemployed but with a research scholarship and pay related to the military service. The mean income of this group was $2,470 per month. Two immigrants were receiving some kind of financial assistance at the time of the study. Only one immigrant had children, others had no

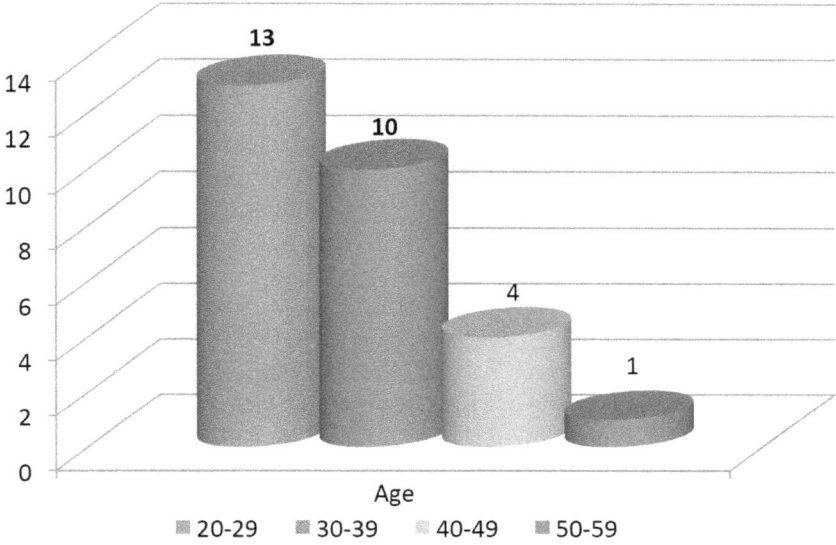

Figure 7.1. Number of Participans by Age

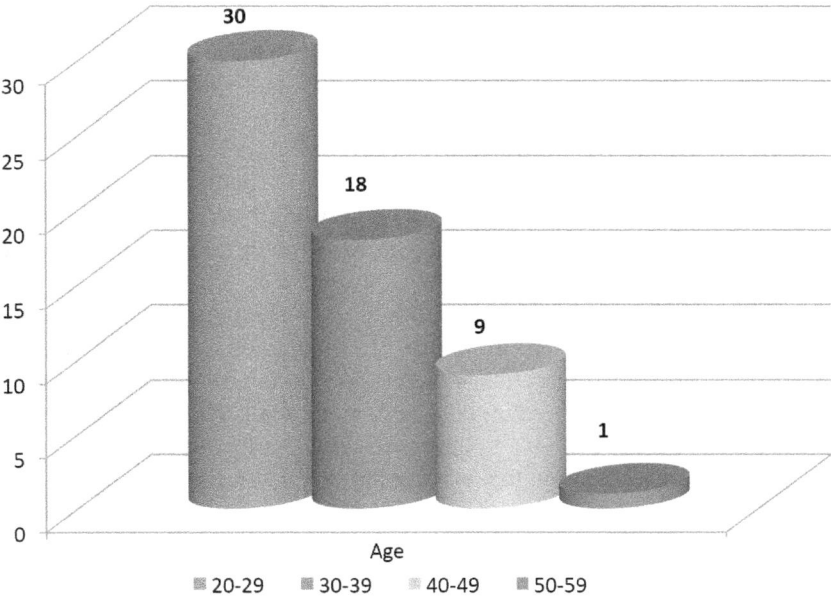

Figure 7.2. Number of All Potential Participants (those who engaged in GCMF but refused to be interviewed) by Age

children or dependents. Five had health insurance and five did not have any coverage.

Six immigrants earned college degrees (three had Master's degrees and three had Bachelor's degrees), three had some college education (but no degree), and one had only 12th grade plus vocational training. Three immigrants were currently enrolled in college at the time of the study. This indicates that interviewed immigrants were better educated than national average (Camille and Bauman, 2015).[3] Additionally, immigrants stated that they had never engaged in any illegal activity, other than the GCMF.

Out of 27 U.S. citizens who participated in GCMF and who were targeted during snowball sampling, 18 agreed to be interviewed (67 percent). The age of participating citizens spanned from 24 to 55 years, with a mean age of 33 years and five months. Forty-four percent were in their twenties, 31 percent in their thirties, 19 percent in their forties, and 6 percent in their fifties.

Within this group were five males and 13 females. Four participants were Caucasian, 10 were African Americans, and three identified themselves as two or more races. Three participants identified themselves as Latino.

With respect to the group of U.S. citizens who were interviewed, 10 had full-time employment, two had part-time employment, one had temporary work, and five were unemployed. Mean income of this group was $1,057 per month. Six citizens were receiving some kind of governmental financial assistance at the time of the study. Thirteen participating citizens had children[4] (five out of 13 had three children or more), four had no children, and one had no children but was in advanced pregnancy. All 17 citizens had health insurance.

Three citizens had college degrees (two had Master's degree and one a Bachelor's degree), 10 declared they did some college but did not graduate, four had a high school diploma or GED, and one had completed the 12th grade only. Three U.S. citizens were still enrolled in college at the time of the study.

Additionally, four U.S. citizens admitted that they had committed a crime in the past (not related to GCMF). One participant confessed to having several charges relating to narcotics and "weapons violations."[5] One participant was charged with aggravated assault, and another was charged with possession of illegal substances. One interviewee also admitted to having had some criminal charges but refused to answer what crime she engaged in.

Immigrants participating in this study overall had much better financial situations than the U.S. citizens. Immigrants had more than two times greater monthly income, and they were more likely to have a full-time job, though at the same time they were seven times less likely to have dependents. However, their average monthly income of $2,472 was still almost twice as low as the mean income in 2015 for the general population (U.S. Census, PINC-01, 2015).[6] On the other hand, the situation of U.S. citizens was much better in regard to health care. At the time of the study, all interviewed citizens had health insurance while only half of the immigrants did. The majority of interviewed citizens had state sponsored affordable health care coverage. This is the insurance to which immigrants have limited access.

BACKGROUND INFORMATION

The basic driving forces of migration are rooted in the differential between the economic situations in the home and host countries (in terms of incomes, unemployment, inequalities, poverty, education levels, etc.), as well as the costs associated with migration costs (Harris and Todaro, 1970; Naiditch, Tomini, and Ben Lakhdar, 2015). The responses of the interviewed immigrants confirm these statements. They are representatives of economic migration.

Eight out of 10 immigrants used cost-benefit analysis to justify their migration to the United States. They described the situation in their home country as worse than what they have currently in the United States. They highlighted lack of jobs, educational opportunities, and avenues to make money. Only one immigrant, Jan from Poland, said that he moved to the United States only temporarily to graduate from an American college and to improve his English. One did not state a reason because he came to the United States with parents during his adolescence, so his parents made that decision for him; however, he mentioned that his family decided to move due to economic factors. Additionally, immigrants from Haiti and Columbia considered their countries as dangerous. Safety was as an important push factor to migrate from the homeland.

Foreigners residing in the United States are often financially responsible for their families in their countries of origin. This is an important push factor regarding the decision to migrate (Drachman and Paulino, 2004; Naiditch, Tomini, and Ben Lakhdar, 2015). Seven out of 10 immigrants who participated in this research made a direct connection between their decision to leave their home countries or to engage in GCMF and a need to take care of members of their family. Natalie, a youthful female student from Haiti summarized:

I just try to find a better life so I can help my family. So, that is my main goal.

It is important to mention that many of them still think about their country of origin as their home, and hope to return there one day. Six immigrants expressed their wish to leave the United States when they are ready to retire.

MOTIVATIONS FOR ENGAGING
IN GREEN CARD MARRIAGE FRAUD

The characteristics and background information presented above about GCMF participants, suggest that the immigrants and the U.S. citizens were very different groups. Therefore, it comes as no surprise that their motives for engaging in GCMF were also different.

Immigrants

All 10 immigrants perceived GCMF as the only option available for them to become a legal permanent resident. However, their understanding of "the only option" was ambiguous. Some understood it literally as the only path they knew to legalize their immigration status and others figuratively. The latter immigrants believed that GCMF was the best path to legal status they had or it was the most reasonable under their current circumstances; it did not mean it was their only existing pathway. For six interviewed immigrants, GCMF was, in their opinions, literally the only option available. They were and still are strongly convinced that there was nothing more they could do to remain legally in the United States. Four immigrants were aware of other potentially available options such as change of visa category to tourist visa (B2) or student visa (F1), and Green Card through a job offer, but they thought about those alternatives as something that could not be achieved in their case.

Bruce, who immigrated from Ghana and is now also a U.S. citizen thanks to GCMF, moved to the United States using a J1 visa as a participant of a Work and Travel Program over eight years prior to the interview. According to his visa requirement, Bruce should have left the United States after a maximum of six months. He did not leave. Instead, he engaged in GCMF because, as was the case for other immigrants, he did not see other options available to him. As a college graduate, he wished to have a chance for an employment visa but was strongly convinced this option is available only for science, technology, engineering, and mathematics (STEM) professionals, while he holds a degree in social science. When asked of alternatives to GCMF, Bruce explained:

It is not feasible. And it is very hard and I got to be a professional, is STEM. (. . .) but that's hard, even people with math, science and engineering they don't want to . . . the companies don't want to do it. What it is, for every immigrant or alien you find, you have to make sure they are like ten Americans that won't be able to do that job, so it wasn't easy, [eh] yes! And more, also my undergrad was like a social science course, so there was no way anybody will even look at me, so the STEM thing was out of the table. (. . .) I wasn't a prisoner of war, or I wasn't under any prosecution or anything I don't know what else could I do, that [GCMF] was the only thing on the table to take.

Improvement of one's socioeconomic situation was also a strong push factor to engage in GCMF. However, only two immigrants directly pointed to financial gain as a reason for their marriage with a U.S. citizen. Seven immigrants indirectly referred to advancing their socioeconomic position through access to a broad range of opportunities that were unavailable to them due to previous lack of legal immigration status. They believed that good jobs are inaccessible for unauthorized foreigners because they require a background check and Employment Eligibility Verification (E-verify).[7] Therefore, unauthorized immigrants must narrow their potential job market to small, private businesses that are more interested in obtaining cheap labor than in verifying their eligibility to work. It is the opinion of many immigrants that being able to pass E-verify is almost equivalent to getting a well-paying job. At the time of the interview, six of the immigrants had authorization to work legally in the United States (three of these immigrants were already U.S. citizens, two were Green Card holders, and one person had a work permit) and four did not have work authorizations but were employed. All 10 immigrants disclosed that they had worked without proper authorization at some point in their lives.

Education was also an important motivator for immigrants thinking about engaging in Green Card marriage fraud. Seven immigrants stressed the importance of educational opportunities that come with the Green Card. For four out of the seven, the possibility to enroll in college and get an American degree was a crucial push factor. However, it should be noted that seven out of 10 interviewed immigrants had an experience with college education in their home countries. They had already graduated or came during summer vacation to participate in the student exchange program, Work and Travel. Therefore, it is not surprising that they have a strong commitment to continue or advance their education in the United States.

Three immigrants mentioned health insurance as an important factor that pushed them into a Green Card marriage fraud. The prospects of out of pocket expenses for health care services raised the level of insecurity. Three spoke about being tired of hiding, of being scared, and being in the shadows; they referred to the constant fear of the possibility of being caught, punished, and consequently deported. The fear was having an impact on their lives and psychological well-being.

Also, three immigrants were partially motivated by their commitment to financially support family members left in their home country or even a desire to bring them to the United States. Two interviewees highlighted the dangerous situation in their home countries as an indirect factor encouraging GCMF. Safety concerns prevented them from returning to their home country. Since return was not possible and their immigration status did not allow adjustment to legal residency, Green Card marriage became justifiable. Other motives that were raised during the interview included: freedom to travel, desire to own a business, and feeling like a sinner.

To sum up, the decision-making process that led immigrants to engage in GCMF was never described as easy or motivated by a single factor. When the interviewed immigrants were asked about motives to enter GCMF, their explanations were complex. All of them considered Green Card marriage wrong but to differing extents. Some felt they disappointed God, and others that they disappointed themselves. Yet others believed they were doing a bad thing but felt that the unique situation they found themselves in excused their action. Most of the interviewees answered similarly to Vladimir, who said:

> *I can list, like, couple main reasons. Firstly, of course money. You know, I can work legally; I can get better job opportunities. Another one is safety, more safety. If you buy car, if you buy home, you feel sure that no one is going to deport you [you will not lose your belonging]. You can do legal things. You can live legally, you can do legal things. Of course, health insurance, medical health care is extremely expensive here . . . And by getting a Green Card I can get insurance and. . . . Yeah, that's pretty related to the safety. And of course, job opportunities.*

Research shows that all interviewed immigrants admitted to wrongdoing but tried to excuse their behavior by mentally asserting that this wrong behavior was actually normative. This is an example of how techniques of neutralization alter the participants' perceptions of GCMF (as a crime).

U.S. Citizens

The driving forces behind the decision of U.S. citizens to engage in GCMF were simpler than the explanations provided by the immigrants. Fifteen Americans stated that the main reason why they decided to participate in this fraudulent activity was for financial gain, indicating their highly disadvantaged economic situation at the time of decision making.

The financial gain received by the U.S. citizens was in cash and in the form of other benefits. David, a single father, was living in a shelter with his one-year-old daughter when a broker approached with an offer for him to marry an African immigrant. As part of the agreement, his future wife was to pay apartment rent and related expenses for himself and his daughter for the duration of their sham marriage. Three years later, at the time of the interview, David was already divorced and living with his four-year-old-child. He had no contact with his ex-wife but he still lived in the same apartment she rented for him and proudly stated that he keeps up with all payments by himself. According to him, the fraudulent marriage gave him an opportunity to be back on his feet.

Rob's financial situation was unstable. He was doing temporary jobs in various fields, whenever something became available. Financial gain in exchange for his participation in GCMF was the strongest incentive for Rob. However, he saw greater potential in this financial gain than the cash that he received. His socioeconomic situation was always challenging, having never had a bank account or credit line. Moreover, he never officially owned anything under his name. But Rob dreamed of owning a construction business. He wanted to *"buy a ran-down house, fix it up, sell it with profit, and buy the next one, and keep going like that."* In order to fulfill his dream, he had to purchase his first house; however, he could not save any money from his temporary jobs. Rob felt that he won't be able to find any permanent employment. He had no chance for a bank loan because he had no credit history. Consequently, he wanted to be sure that the lack of his financial history would be addressed. His African wife was stable financially and she agreed to purchase a vehicle for herself and include her new husband in the loan plan. She also opened a joint bank account and promised to keep it active. The newlyweds also agreed to have a shared phone account and life insurance. All these shared items would help the couple to prove the authenticity of their marriage to USCIS officers. Moreover, it would help Rob to build a financial history for obtaining a sufficient credit rating in order to start his business. He knew it would take a few years, so in the meantime he wanted to become a full-time Uber driver and start saving money. Likewise, this activity would not be possible without the support of his wife. Rob saw his marriage as a life changing event for uplifting his socioeconomic prospects.

Surprisingly, the second most frequently presented purpose for engaging in marriage fraud was very altruistic and not a rationale that had been considered in preparing this research. According to 12 interviewed U.S. citizens, the possibility of helping someone in need (future spouse) to better their life was one of the crucial push factors in deciding to marry an immigrant. Three out of 12 interviewees said that this reason was more important than any other. Interviewed citizens repeatedly expressed a lack of understanding or acceptance of current immigration laws and regulations and felt that foreigners are treated unfairly. Juana explained why she married an immigrant in the following words:

To be honest the main reason was because of the lack of opportunity. The person that I have decided to marry didn't have the opportunity to study; because his main goal was to study science (. . .). Here I am a person that is citizen and wouldn't even study–because I'm into career. So, to me it was like: wow, this guy actually really wants to study! (. . .) But you have people that just lack it [will to study] and just let it go to waste.

Paula was led to Green Card marriage by a combination of financial and altruistic factors. She recalled her decision-making process in the following words:

He was from the Dominican Republic. And then, I was like getting to know him a little bit, and then he was talking about his struggles and his situation but I . . . of course I was gonna get something out of it, you know . . . the whole point of offering money; I was gonna get financial compensation. So, it wasn't like 'oh yes, let's do this for this guy' and that's it. No. We just talked about it and I feel bad about his situation, he had no papers, he didn't see his kids in years, They were still in Dominican Republic, he couldn't travel to see them, and I thought about his kids; he did have two (2) kids. He was always talking about them. And I feel little moved by that and wanted to help but then, you know, but the main reason for marrying him was money, of course. Because if it wasn't money involved I wasn't gonna do it but, yea, it was money. And then I was like . . . I have dependents. Yea. Back in the days I had not only the two (2) that I have now but I had four (4) children. So, I thought that I can make some money out of this.

Multiple times, citizens complemented their foreign-spouses for their academic achievements and willingness to learn and work hard. Moreover, they often compared themselves to their spouses in a manner that suggested the superiority of their spouses in the areas of education, employment, socioeconomic status, or even behavior and morals. Therefore, in their opinion it was unfair that immigration law does not grant permission to stay in the United States to those who present such high standards.

In many cases, compassion and will to help were enhanced by stories told to U.S. citizens by their future spouses about violations of human rights, wars, extreme poverty, or natural disasters in their home countries. Lori, a U.S. citizen, was proud of being able to help two African immigrants. *"When you help somebody, you get blessed"*—she repeated this sentence multiple times like a mantra. Lori explained:

You can't be cruel and cold-hearted to people because they're from another state. (. . .) If I gotta get somebody married so they can get their family from there [home country], that be the main thing. Because they have kids. And then I see on TV the kids that starve and stuff like that. You know what I mean? Like, get the kids over here and get them a better life. It's more about the kids and majority of the people we deal with have families. So . . . just gotta help people (. . .). They're human beings. They're not savages. They're not animals.

Lori heard many stories from her immigrant-husband about the life in his home country—Rwanda. It strongly influenced her will to engage in fraud marriage(s). Another U.S. citizen, Joe, also felt sympathy for those in need. He heard from his uncle stories about a girl from a country destroyed by a natural disaster. The girl was looking for the opportunity to stay in a safe country. Compassion associated with the natural disaster affected Joe's decision to engage in GCMF.

Family or friends' influence was also an important factor that pushed some citizens into GCMF(s). Only three people stated it directly as an answer to the question about the reason they engaged in marriage fraud. However, when interviewees were asked how they were introduced to GCMF, they provided many stories highlighting strong influence of their family members and friends. Despite that fact, citizens had a problem with classifying this influence as a purpose of their engagement in fraud.

Yolanda was deeply in love with her boyfriend Carlos who unexpectedly propositioned her about marrying an immigrant in exchange for money. A few years before, Carlos himself participated in GCMF and married a Guatemalan immigrant. After a successful transaction,[8] the marriage fraud broker who introduced Carlos to GCMF asked him to work for her and recruit U.S. citizens willing to participate in GCMF. Carlos agreed. Yolanda says, she was the fourth person he successfully recruited. When he asked her to get involved in GCMF, Yolanda did not agree right away. He kept talking about it and explaining the financial benefits until she was convinced. Yolanda explained her reason for entering GCMF in the following words: "*I was nineteen at that time and I was in love with the person. So, I was set to do . . . like, whatever he asked.*" Carlos was helping the marriage fraud broker to find U.S. citizens willing to engage in marriage fraud. His work was very similar to what Lori described in subchapter *Facilitation of Green Card marriage fraud.* For every U.S. citizen introduced to the broker and successfully married,[9] the broker paid him six hundred dollars ($600). However, the time when Carlos involved his girlfriend in the business, he decided to double his profits. As always, he received six hundred dollars ($600) from the broker for bringing Yolanda to her but he also charged Yolanda six hundred dollars ($600) for giving her the opportunity to get married and make money. Yolanda was convinced that all participants were charged the same amount, and that this was the way the fraud marriage business was ran. She was not surprised when her boyfriend asked to be paid for his service. Yolanda gave him his part of the money as soon as she received the money from her new husband.

Trice, a U.S. citizen, was convinced to engage in GCMF by her relatives. Two of her cousins were already married to immigrants. She described her financial situation by the time she met her future husband as "good." She was working and keeping financial balance. As much as the possibility to make easy money was appealing to her, it was not a necessity. Her family used their authority and trust to get her into the business. Trice believed her family recommended GCMF to her because they knew it was a beneficial option for her. She believed in their honest intentions, even though she was aware that her relatives were paid for bringing her into the business. Trice said:

> *They [cousins] actually talked to me about it first. And you know, told me what they did and wanted to see if I was maybe interested and want try it. They wanted to see if I was interested in it and wanted to help me improve my financial situation. Basically they talk to me about it first, they told me about what they did, they told me about green card helping someone else so they can stay here [in the United States]. [. . .] I know my cousins got paid for me getting into it [GCMF]. But I am not sure the exact amount. Few hundred. But they were also some other people involved. They also got paid. So I can't get to the bottom of it, who got a share of my money. I stopped asking.*

In general, financial gain (in a monetary form or valuable items) was a main reason why U.S. citizens engaged in GCMF despite possible severe consequences. According to rational choice theory, "crimes are broadly the result of rational choices based on analyses of anticipated cost and benefits" (Cornish and Clarke, 1986, p. vi). U.S. citizens enter GCMF as a business transaction. They calculate potential profits and losses, often negotiate the amount of their gain, and some even have written agreements with their spouses regarding payments and the responsibilities of both sides.[10]

Marriage Fraud Brokers

Marriage fraud brokers had similar reasons to arrange fraud marriages as U.S. citizens did to participate in them. Elizabeth was very clear that her only purpose to arrange Green Card marriages was money. However, when Naomi was asked for her motives to engage in fraud marriages, she stated:

> *I'm a bookie, I do my part, I don't agree with anything that the states does to these people [immigrants], I don't think it's fair to work a job hard as hell and have the least amount of money because you don't have a piece of paper or a work permit, I don't think it's right, I don't think it's right that you go to school,*

*you work your hardest and you go somewhere else and it means nothing, I have
a problem with it.*

Even though she was well paid for arranging marriages (details of the transactions are subject of following subchapters), Naomi described her main reason for participating in marriage fraud as "helping others." She spoke a lot about her compassion for the situation of immigrants in the United States. Her current husband graduated from medical school and was working as a doctor in Nigeria. In order to practice medicine in the United States, he had to return to medical school in the U.S. Naomi was moved that after such extensive education and practice in his home country, he could not work as a doctor in the United States. She said, "*he meant nothing*" here. After receiving a medical degree from the American college, his visa expired, and he was expected to return to his country. But he wanted to stay in the U.S. and practice medicine here. That was when marriage with a U.S. citizen became a viable option. He was the third African immigrant who Naomi married for the purpose of evading the immigration laws. She spoke highly of all of them and felt they were not treated fairly by the system.

Steven, the only immigrant among three brokers, was motivated by a combination of financial benefits and the will to help people who found themselves in a situation similar to his own. He highlighted that arranging Green Card marriages is an easy and effective way to make money. However, he also "*want[s] to help [his] fellow Nigerians and students.*" Steven overstayed his J1 visa and in an attempt to legalize his status, decided to marry a U.S. citizen. His knowledge about immigration law was not sufficient to successfully complete the process and receive the Green Card. The Marriage Fraud broker who arranged his marriage was not helpful and did not guide him through the process. Nonetheless, applying for a Green Card (although ineffective), helped him to finish college. Steven sacrificed a lot to receive a Master's degree and was very proud of it. He remembered how powerless he was during the GCMF process; therefore, he was especially glad when he could help someone who was striving to get an education. He wants people to get better guidelines than he received from his broker. Steven shed light on the issue of engaging in GCMF even when knowing the Green Card will be denied. He said:

You are looking at the Green Card marriages statistics and you see that majority of the marriages is approved. Then you look at those not approved and you hope the system is doing its job by targeting fake marriages. But not so fast. Between those rejected are many winners. Sometimes I get a client and I know from the start he won't get it. He doesn't have his ducks in order, or his budget is very tight, so I know we won't get a proper girl out of that. Once I got 45-years old lesbian for this nice 22-years old student. It couldn't work. But you see, when you get married and apply for your Green Card, you can also submit your I-765[11] and it will come fast, usually in a month or two. That moment you can go and apply for social security number, you can get your ID or driver's license, you can get health insurance; and you have a work permit for a year or two, or as long as your case is pending. And even you fail your Green Card interview, they won't take away your ID and they won't cancel your social security number. You can still get a job if you have these two documents. You see what I mean? You can't travel but you are paroled as long as your case is rolling, and they can't deport you. You have long time to figure out your next step.

The explanation provided by Steven revealed that some immigrants may approach GCMF as an avenue to become eligible to apply for an ID or driver's license, social security number, and temporary work authorization. Those, whose Green Card cases are pending, are eligible to apply for a permit to temporarily leave the United States (Form I-131, Application for Travel Document) (USCIS, 2020b).[12] Immigrants may not make an effort to prove bona fide marriage to the USCIS officials. Some are satisfied with what they get—most of all, the opportunity to apply for legal employment and documents that legalize important daily activities such as driving a vehicle.

Another broker, Elizabeth, also commented on this issue:

"Sometimes immigrants don't get lucky with their spouses, you know. Sometimes they get someone who really hustle them for money. Or someone who doesn't care about their success with the Green Card. It can be hard, and they get tired. You know, it's draining, mentally. So they say, fine! I've got my [driver's] license, I've got my work papers, so I don't need this crap anymore. I can live like that. I don't need this stress." Later she added *"So I am satisfied. They bettered their life. Maybe not the way they planned it but it got better, so I am cool with that."*

None of the three marriage fraud brokers expressed regrets for arranging fraud marriages or plan to discontinue this activity. They saw both positive (financial gain, helping others) and negative (risk of being caught and punished) sides of this activity but stated that they were not willing to stop. Among U.S. citizens participating in marriage fraud, only one regretted her decision and would not repeat that behavior in the future. Two others regretted that they did not take control of how the GCMF was arranged and organized or regretted that they agreed to marry their spouse without getting to know the person in advance. They stated that they might agree to marry an immigrant in exchange for financial gain in the future, if the process was to be organized differently. On the other hand, within the group of 10 interviewed immigrants, three regretted their actions and felt the burden of their wrongdo-ing. Two referred to Catholic beliefs as a root of their regrets. Jan said:

I felt bad because I am an honest person and I don't want to lie. I felt like, I did something wrong. [. . .] I felt bad inside with this and I didn't want to lie in courts. I have felt bad. I am a Catholic and Catholic Church doesn't recognize the civil marriage but I still think that civil marriage is not the way to get a busi-ness done. I didn't want to treat marriage as a way to do business.

Francis felt that the decision to engage in GCMF changed him as a person and influenced the way he interacts with other people. He said:

I do regret. Up to this day, I do. I feel sometimes it [GCMF] has actually shelled me and made me a little bit cautious about opening up about my life to other people. I feel like, I am vulnerable when I share my life with people. Like, especially before, when I was still married to the other girl [GCMF wife], you know, it was hard to tell people ok, I am married. Because I did not want to put up with questions, who is your wife? Where is your wife? You know, yeah. I had this interesting experience when I was working in a big lab and I actual met a gentleman who was interested in my academics and he was happy to lead me. He said, oh ok I am gonna try to see if we can find you a job in our lab and all that. You know, I got my shot. Someone noticed me. And then he learned I didn't have my papers, so we talked, and I was honest. I'm like, ok my wife is working on it for me and all that. And he said 'oh you're married? What's your wife name? What does your wife do?' I'm like, oh she is still looking for a job. And the girl [GCMF wife] was actually looking for a job then. So a week or two later, this person comes to tell me that he really wants to help me, he wants to talk to my wife and he says their office has need for an assistance and he might be able to hook my wife up. So, I broke. I cannot forget how I felt that day. I can't, seriously [sighs heavily]. I couldn't live the life of lie around this person, who pretty much wanted to became my mentor and offered his help. You know, so I pretty much had to let him know. And I did. I told him, this is my situation

KNOWLEDGE ABOUT LEGAL CONSEQUENCES OF GREEN CARD MARRIAGE FRAUD

The "cash-for-vows" type of fraud marriage always involves at least two offenders—the two spouses who enter a marriage to evade the immigration laws of the United States. Both spouses, an immigrant and a U.S. citizen, may face the legal consequences of their actions. GCMF is a federal crime and according to the *Immigration and Nationality Act*, "Any individual who knowingly enters into a marriage for the purpose of evading any provision of the immigration laws shall be imprisoned for not more than five years, or fined not more than $250,000, or both" (I.N.A. Section 275(c)). Additionally, a foreign national can be placed in the process of deportation based on 8 U.S. Code § 1227(a)(1)(G). If he or she still holds a nonimmigrant (temporary) visa, it can be revoked. The record of marriage fraud would remain on the person's immigration record forever, making it virtually impossible to obtain a Green Card in the future or even a nonimmigrant United States visa (ICE, 2014). Moreover, those who are spouses can also be convicted for violation of, or an attempt or a conspiracy to violate, section 1546 of Title 18 (relating to fraud and misuse of visas, permits, and other entry documents, and making false statements under oath).[13]

Severe civil and criminal consequences of marriage fraud should successfully deter potential offenders. However, research exposes that participants' knowledge of these consequences is generally minimal or inaccurate. When Ashley, U.S. citizen, was asked about her knowledge of GCMF consequences, she answered:

> *I know it's severe. That's why we made sure everything went through. And he actually . . . because I was scared for a while, we did bunch of fraud things and . . . I didn't want to get to details. He [husband] took care of everything. I really don't want to know how severe it was. I basically jumped into more before I knew the consequences. That's why I didn't wanna know because I was already in it. And I don't want to know now.*

Eight out of 17 interviewed citizens and seven out of ten immigrants admitted to having no knowledge of the consequences of GCMF. Nine citizens and three immigrants stated that they were aware of the potential penalties for their involvement in marriage fraud. However, within this group, only three citizens and one immigrant expected a penalty similar to that provided by law.[14] Eight out of 10 immigrants mentioned deportation as a penalty for fraud marriage. Also, three U.S. citizens expected to be deported from the United States if convicted of GCMF. Moreover, one U.S. citizen suspected that she "*won't be allowed to marry again*" if convicted.

The research revealed that U.S. citizens were less afraid of potential consequences for their participation in GCMF than immigrants. Only five interviewed citizens feared consequences of GCMF. The remaining 12 stated that they were not afraid of being arrested and charged with GCMF or they did not think about it. On the other hand, all interviewed immigrants were afraid of being caught. However, their main fear was deportation and lack of future opportunity to return to the United States, not imprisonment or fines.

Consequences for GCMF brokers are more severe. For engaging in conspiracy operations, they can be sentenced to a maximum term of 25 years. Two marriage fraud brokers did not know what the legal consequences are for engaging in GCMF. Additionally, both added that they *"don't want to know"* what these consequences are. One marriage fraud broker expected that if caught and prosecuted, she could face imprisonment for about five years and a ten thousand dollar ($10,000) fine. She knew that there was a chance she might be caught and was prepared to deal with the consequences. The other two marriage fraud brokers stated that they were afraid of being caught and explained that the fear is continuous.[15]

While rational choice theory states that people weigh the risks and benefits of committing a crime, it does not assume that their evaluation of the risks is based on accurate information. Poor or inaccurate knowledge of the consequences of GCMF did not prevent participants from making rational choices. All but one participant, a U.S. citizen, understood that they had engaged in a criminal behavior punishable by law. Therefore, by participating in GCMF they accepted. risks of potential punishment in order to benefit from this crime.

Facilitation of Green Card Marriage Fraud

Immigrants can become undocumented by unauthorized entry, by staying beyond the expiration date of their status or other authorization, or by violating the terms of legal entry. All ten immigrant interviewees in this study entered the United States lawfully through the port of entry (in all cases airports) on a temporary visa. Five immigrants entered the United States on J1 visa (exchange visitors),[16] two entered on F1 visa (academic students),[17] and three entered on B2 visa (visitor).[18,19] Nine out of 10 participants married their American spouses when their visa had already expired, and their status turned into "unauthorized alien." Only one participant got married before the expiration of her visa. She visited the United States to participate in the cultural exchange program and returned to her country of origin as scheduled.[20] The following year, she signed up for the same program and entered the United States as an exchange visitor. However, this time she did not return home at the end of the program but engaged in GCMF. She had already prepared herself for this move during her first visit; therefore, it was possible for her to complete her plan before the expiration of the visa.

All 10 immigrants confirmed that their life improved after official immigration to the United States. However, half of the interviewees (at the time of the interview) did not succeed in receiving a Green Card and still struggled with the consequences of their illegal immigration status. Two immigrants had already become U.S. citizens through a process called naturalization, another two were legal permanent residents, and one had a valid visa and work permit. The remaining five immigrants overstayed their visas and had no legal immigration status. All 10 interviewees believed GCMF was the only available way to improve their lives.

The Initiation Process

Thirteen out of 17 citizens and eight out of 10 immigrants were assisted by marriage fraud brokers. However, brokers were not always direct recruiters of citizens. All of the interviewed immigrants learned of the possibility of engaging in GCMF from friends or family members who are already U.S. citizens or permanent residents. The process of introduction was very similar for all interviewed immigrants. Family or friends stepped into the role of advisers for newcomers, discussing social life, employment, immigration procedures, and applicable laws in a greater context. Immigrant communities have developed a certain way of dealing with unsupportive (for many) immigration law. Often, family members or friends made arrangements with marriage fraud brokers immediately after the new immigrant arrived in the United States, or sometimes even before he or she arrived. The help they offered was usually free and altruistic, and the only goal they had was to help newcomers to succeed. Moreover, due to cultural considerations, immigrant communities immigrant communities had a certain way of doing things.[21] When new immigrants joined the community, they were not only offered advice but also expected to take it. Eight out of ten interviewed immigrants were introduced by friends or family members to a marriage fraud broker. The remaining two were introduced directly to their future spouse. Communities developed relationships with brokers and introduced all their newcomers to that particular broker. Therefore, it was observed that brokers specialized in serving people of a particular background. For example, Naomi focused on recruiting mostly West Africans, especially Nigerians.

Citizens interviewed for this research who participated in GCMF were usually recruited by friends or family members. However, the particular reasons for initiating new people into the "Green Card business" were not always of an altruistic (typically unpaid) nature, as it was in the case of immigrants. Thirteen interviewed Americans were navigated through the process by brokers. Seven of them were recruited by family or friends who introduced them to the broker. Between those seven, four said that people who introduced them to brokers were paid for this activity. One person was sure that her best friend did not get paid for "*hooking her up*" with the broker, and two other participants were not sure if their friends got paid. With regard to the recruitment process, one case was unusual—Joe's case.

Joe was a college student in his twenties when his uncle approached him with the idea to marry an immigrant girl. Joe's uncle developed the marriage plan with an aunt of the wife-to-be. The idea of GCMF was not new to Joe because his brother and cousin were already involved in it (also thanks to the uncle). Both of them—brother and cousin—were paid for participating in marriage fraud but in Joe's case, the uncle chose different arguments than money. He wanted Joe to help the girl. Joe recalled:

[. . .] Uncle said why won't you just help her get into the country. So I thought why not. [. . .] At that time they had a natural disaster over there in [country of origin]. It destroyed everything over there.

Joe agreed to help by marrying the young woman. She received her Green Card, but payment for this transaction was divided between Joe's uncle and the immigrant wife's aunt. Joe received no financial gain.

Those Americans who successfully went through the GCMF process and developed a positive relationship with the broker were often asked to help recruit more Americans. That is how Lori described the recruitment process:

Well, I most likely probably know the girls, so it's not hard to find a girl. If you have a million friends that are broke . . . honestly, you know, they broke–they broke, and some people are hungry for money. So some people will do whatever they wanna do, or do what they got to do to survive out here. Because it's a cruel world, you know. So if she needs somebody at a certain age, I may can help her [broker]. I can't help her all the time because sometimes I have no . . . I have people that they haven't got the age requirement that they've been looking, sometimes. But most likely I do, pretty much have a lot of friends [. . .].

Lori was paid five hundred dollars ($500) for every person she successfully recruited.

The next six participants knew the brokers directly and referred to them as friends. Brokers themselves highlighted that in their jobs it is important to maintain a wide circle of friends. They knew many people and considered themselves to be known by many.

Four American participants got to know their future spouse without the help of the broker. Their stories were unique. Two American females met their future Green-Card-husbands unexpectedly and in casual environments. Paula met her husband in a club and Shelly at work. In both cases, women got to know the men, became friends with them, and shortly after were introduced to the idea of getting married in exchange for financial gain. Interestingly, even though the fraud was conceived between these friends and co-workers, when the decision about GCMF was made, they still engaged a marriage broker in the process. Shelly was friends with the broker and she was told that without a broker their case would fail. She convinced her husband that a broker was necessary in order for her to feel comfortable and continue with the process.

The third woman, Anna, was introduced to her future husband by her extended family and friends. As every summer, she had joined her family to work in the family-owned business. Her future husband was working there already, and proved to be a very committed and reliable employee. Anna's family did not want to lose such a good worker (which would happen if he had to go back to his home in Serbia) and they decided to help him find a wife in order to be eligible to apply for permanent residency. Anna agreed to become his wife.

The last interviewed woman who arranged the marriage without a broker was introduced to her husband by her friends who were also friends of her future husband. These friends wanted to help their male friend stay in the country, while helping Juana make extra income during a period of financial challenge. Juana's friends had engaged in GCMF themselves, and saw it as the only chance for the man to stay in the country. That is how she thought about the situation of her future husband. Her friends presented the process in a very tempting way, so Juana could not resist and agreed to participate.

NOTES

1. According to the U.S. Census (2018) two or more races refers to combinations of two or more of the following race categories: "White," "Black or African American," American Indian or Alaska Native," "Asian," Native Hawaiian or Other Pacific Islander," or "Some Other Race."

2. Potential participants are individuals who participated in GCMF targeted during snowball sampling; this group includes those who participated in the interview and those who refused.

3. In 2015, almost nine out of 10 adults (88 percent) had at least a high school diploma or GED, while nearly one in three adults (33 percent) held a Bachelor's or higher degree.

4. None have had children with the immigrant spouse.

5. Later it was clarified that interviewee meant the unlawful possession of a firearm.

6. Census money income is defined as income received on a regular basis (exclusive of certain money receipts such as capital gains) before payments for personal

income taxes, social security, union dues, Medicare deductions, etc. The mean total income for 2015 was $44,510 a year or $3,709 a month.

7. Under federal law, E-Verify is voluntary for all employers with exceptions for federal government employers and violators of certain immigration laws that are ordered to participate. However, 20 states enacted laws requiring mandatory use of E-Verify by some or all state and local agencies, state and local contractors, and even certain private businesses.

8. Guatemalan immigrant received a Green Card and the couple divorced immediately after that fact.

9. The money was paid immediately after the marriage ceremony, when all parties were assured that the marriage took place as planned.

10. Most of those who mentioned written agreements understand that due to the illegal nature of Green Card marriage they cannot use it in court to force their spouse to pay the agreed amount. But two interviewed U.S. citizens believe they have a right to sue their spouses if they will not follow the rules discussed in the written agreement.

11. Form I-765 is an Application for Employment Authorization, to request employment authorization and an Employment Authorization Document (EAD).

12. Steven did not mention the possibility to apply for a permit to travel. This point is added by the author.

13. More information on legal consequences of GCMF is provided in Chapter 3.

14. These participants explained that the penalty for GCMF included imprisonment for a period of about five years. Three citizens also mentioned a fine.

15. There was a noticeable difference in the marriage fraud brokers' fear level, perceived by the interviewer during the interviews. The two marriage fraud brokers who had no knowledge of the consequences of GCMF were more reluctant to be interviewed and were more reserved during the interview. The marriage fraud brokers who had knowledge of the consequences of GCMF were more comfortable and open during the interview. However, all three marriage fraud brokers did not want to talk about the chances of being caught, penalties, and the other people they know who have been charged with involvement in GCMF. They expressed unpleasant feelings during this part of the interview (using different expressions such as: uncomfortable, anxious, afraid; or repeating "I don't want to think about this").

16. J1 status is for those who intend to participate in an approved program for the purpose of teaching, instructing or lecturing, studying, observing, conducting research, consulting, demonstrating special skills, receiving training, or to receive graduate medical education or training (USCIS, 2015).

17. The F1 visa allows a person to enter the United States as a full-time student at an accredited college, university, seminary, conservatory, academic high school, elementary school, or other academic institution or in a language training program (USCIS, 2016).

18. Visitor visas are nonimmigrant visas for persons who want to enter the United States temporarily for tourism, pleasure or visiting (DHS, 2018).

19. A male immigrant from the Caribbean migrated when he was a teen and his parents were in charge of his legal documents. He entered the United States by plane and had a visa but he is not sure what kind. He said: "*I applied for visa. I'm not sure*

. . . they [parents] *had something, travel visa probably and I just overstayed, or something like that."* I count this case as B2 visa entry.

20. The most popular program of international cultural exchange that allows students from different countries to undertake summer travel to the United States is for work. The program is supervised by the U.S. Department of State.

21. Groups of people that emigrated from the same country or neighboring country.

Chapter Eight

Fraudulent Transactions and Documentation

This chapter describes various preliminary steps, broker transactions, and the organized crime aspects associated with Green Card marriage fraud (GCMF). In particular, the actual wedding arrangements such as marriage price negotiations as well as wedding day practices are described. Other matters discussed include the tricks used to deceive immigration officials, especially the types of false documentation produced to ostensibly prove the existence of a valid marital relationship. In addition, the distinctive roles of marriage fraud brokers and others involved in scheming to commit Green Card marriage fraud are considered.

WEDDING ARRANGEMENTS

In the perpetration of GCMF, the first official step is for the immigrant and a U.S. citizen to get married. The interviews revealed that the future spouses rarely make an effort to get to know each other in advance. The interviewees' statements suggested that they thought about their future interpersonal union as a business agreement rather than promise to live together in the relationship. Nine interviewed U.S. citizens and eight immigrants directly called their marriage "*a business.*" When Vladimir was asked if he ever engaged in any romantic or intimate situation with his spouse, he answered: "*It was a clear business, no romantic situations at all.*" Natalie also drew a clear line between a romantic relationship and the Green Card marriage arrangement. Her answer to the same question was as follows: "*I never really found him attractive. I'm just this kind of person—business is business.*" The marriage ceremony itself was also often described as a business transaction. Naomi described her ceremony in the following words: "*So when that process take place it's kinda quick. it's really not a social event–more business.*"

Brokers usually organized one or two meetings before the marriage ceremony, during which the immigrant and U.S. citizen actually saw each other for the first time. According to all three interviewed brokers, future spouses usually met twice before their wedding day. Participants themselves had various experiences. While some individuals knew each other before the marriage, five of them (three immigrants and two U.S. citizens) did not meet their spouse until the day of their wedding ceremony. In all of these cases, the broker or friend arranged the meeting a few hours before the planned ceremony so they could personally discuss essential details. Two participants met their future spouses only once before the wedding day. Eleven people were able to arrange two or three pre-nuptial meetings. Five participants had gotten to know their future spouses for one or two months, and four participants for three to six months.

All ceremonies described by participants were performed by an in-state justice of the peace.[1] None of the marriages were performed by clergy or a specially designated "justice of the peace for-a-day."

The Massachusetts State law required couples to file the Notice of Intention of Marriage at least three days before their wedding (M.G.L. ch. 207, § 19) and the marriage license customarily will not be issued until at least the third day from the filing of the notice (M.G.L. ch. 207, §28). However, such a waiting period can be waived by filing a request for a Marriage without Delay with the state district court or probate court (M.G.L. ch. 207, §30). Eight interviewees obtained a waiver of the three-day notice period and married the same day. Obviously, this number includes all five participants who stated that they were introduced to their spouse on the wedding day. The other three interviewees participated in one to three meetings with their future spouse before the wedding day. The remaining 19 participants scheduled their wedding in advance.

All 27 interviewees who had engaged in GCMF were asked how they would describe their wedding day. The most common epithets stated to describe the ceremonies were: "fast," "quick," "weird," "unreal," "crazy," and "unromantic." They described their feelings during the ceremony as: "nervous," "anxious," and "awkward." One American female stated that she wore a white wedding gown. Four participants (three U.S. citizens and one immigrant) highlighted that they dressed elegantly and the rest casual. The following descriptions of clothes were classified as elegant: "long dress," "evening dress," "white women suit," or when participants directly described his/her dress code as elegant. Descriptions of casual wear included a wide range of outfits, such as "nice jeans and blouse,'" "nice shirt," "better clothes," "normal t-shirt," "shorts and flip flops" or clothes described by participants as normal or casual.

Sixteen participants exchanged wedding rings after they said their vows. However, four of them emphasized that their rings did not have the value of traditional wedding rings, describing them as "not real," "plastic," "'metal," "very cheap," and "Walmart rings." Eight participants stated that they did not exchange wedding rings and the remaining three did not remember or did not answer the question. In an effort to make their marriage commitment look genuine, 12 interviewees followed the standard married name-change tradition and took their spouse's last name or allowed their spouse to have his/her last name. Another 12 individuals did not change their last name or give their last name to the spouse. Three participants did not answer this question.

After the official marriage ceremony, newlyweds did not follow what might be considered a customary or traditional celebration. Eleven participants stated that immediately after the ceremony they went separate ways. Others spent some time together.[2] Ten newlywed couples went to a restaurant or bar, by themselves or with those who participated in their ceremony. Three couples left the city and stayed together in a hotel or campground. Couples never stayed in the same room or engaged in any kind of romantic or intimate situation. They stressed that it was a necessary outing in order to obtain valuable pictures that were expected to constitute important evidence in their future Green Card application process. The same argument was raised by most of the people who went to a bar or restaurant. Moreover, immigrants wanted to ensure their spouses' future cooperation and treated the outing as an opportunity to build a friendly relationship. The immigrants paid for all outings with their American spouses.

To sum up, GCMF participants reported that they followed the marriage procedure only to the point that it was required by law. Traditional elements are rarely incorporated, and they reported little or no effort to comfort each other in the situation that they considered "stressful and awkward." Tania (an immigrant) provided a full description of the wedding day that reflected well the steps taken by those who enter the marriage to evade the immigration laws.

It was ridiculously funny. I mean, now I think about is as funny but that day it wasn't like that. I was really scared. So we met at 8am that day. They were opening at 9am I guess but the broker wanted to introduce us first and stuff. So we met by the front door and broker propose to go to some breakfast place across the street to talk. We went. They order breakfast. I got coffee only. Of course, they made me pay. So, we spoke about money, how this deal will go. Actually the broker was talking and we were just like "yea, yea, agree" and stuff. So next [. . .] we went to city hall to fill some papers, pay some fees. And

[. . .] we went somewhere across the street to get some license, so we could marry same day. We had to stop on the way and I had to pay via money order some fee for that service. There was something like "mini-hearing" they called us and said we can marry same day. All of that took few hours so was afternoon already. We came back and broker said we will marry with her justice of the peace. So that's were fun began. She drove us to his house. It was like 5 or 6pm already. We got there he asked if we wanna marry by his pool because he has nice patio or inside the house. Broker said house and we went to his living room. I was shocked. I didn't know you can marry in someone's house. I was like asking myself "are they conning me or what the hell?" The justice of peace was in slippers and sport suit. He asked something, like, do we want to say our vows because we don't look like we want and he laugh. So he was like I understand "you do and you also do, I announce you husband and wife, thank you, two fifty ($250)." That's all. We even didn't say vows. He signed the paper we got from city hall or whatever it was. I don't even remember because broker was keeping everything. She told me I really have to pay the guy two hundred fifty ($250) and we left. That was my wedding. They dropped me by train station and I was waiting there for my friend. And broker took my husband.

MARRIAGE PRICE NEGOTIATIONS

Brokers or other third parties (family members or friends) involved in arranging the marriage often mediated the price, responsibilities, and other conditions of the illicit marriage transaction between future spouses. As noted above, 13 out of 17 U.S. citizens and 8 out of 10 immigrants were assisted by marriage fraud brokers. In the case of two citizens, family members negotiated the price with the marriage fraud broker, and the concerned marriage participants were only informed about the price but could not influence it. Eleven U.S. citizens and all eight immigrants personally discussed the price with the marriage fraud broker. Ten citizens and seven immigrants participated in the meeting organized by marriage fraud brokers during which the details of the deal, especially price, were set. All these meetings took place in restaurants and both parties (immigrants and U.S. citizens) were welcome to bring a friend or family member in order to feel more comfortable. In most cases each party brought one additional person.[3]

Steven recalled:

Well, first meeting it's [aaa] . . . the . . . you meet the broker basically, what tend to happened now is that [aaa] you negotiate the price, you tell her the kind of girl you need, age, mostly you wanna say you don't want any with kids, someone who is working, and . . . and be able to sponsor you or anything. So the broker basically is gonna agree to everything you say. However, when the . . . next time you meet a girl you don't know much about her. That is basically where the process already starts. You are gonna get married that particular day.

The price for the marriage spans from two thousand eight hundred dollars ($2,800) to twenty thousand dollars ($20,000), with the average price of eight thousand dollars ($8,000).[4,5] Five U.S. citizens' discussed price included the immigrant spouse paying for living expenses (such as rent, utilities, phone bill, etc.) and/or educational expenses (tuition and books) and/or purchasing valuable items such as a car, smartphone, or laptop. One immigrant also described the financial agreement as involving paying for the future spouse's living expenses. The remaining U.S. citizens and immigrants agreed on the amount that should be paid in cash or periodically deposited into a bank account. However, in the cases of five immigrants, the agreement changed during the marriage and they ended up paying more than was discussed before the marriage. In all five cases, American spouses requested multiple additional payments in between discussed installment rates. Steven, who also paid more than discussed before the marriage ceremony explained:

The agreement wasn't taking about small amounts . . . fifty dollars ($50) here, hundred dollars ($100) here, twenty dollars ($20) here, two hundred dollars ($200) here. No. Supposed to be paid in installment as the process moves forward then I pay part of the money owned her. But, I mean, the process is long, is like approximately eight (8) months before one can even go for an interview. So, within that eight (8) months weekly you're paying . . . she wants fifty dollars ($50) for gas money, for phone bill, for kid want to go out . . . so . . . and that doesn't come out of the agreed sum.

Moreover, five U.S. citizens also stated that the arrangement had changed but in their case for the better. They had received more money than was discussed before the marriage. One of them stated that the immigrant-spouse offered to pay more on their own initiative and without a previous request from the citizen-spouse. The remaining four citizens admitted to asking for additional payments from their immigrant-spouses. For Shelly, these additional payments were an obvious part of the transaction. She said:

He pays my phone bills, he buys diapers, stuff like that for my son, [um] if I need food or something, he just sends money on the side, so . . . of course, there was more money on the side.

When asked what she would do if the husband would not want to provide more money than they discussed before getting married, she answered:

[I] just stop the whole thing [laughter]. Just start over with somebody else . . . you know.

Shelly was not the only one who was ready to use the threat of leaving the Green Card marriage agreement if the spouse was unable or unwilling to provide a satisfactory amount of money.[6] Three other American spouses admitted to using the same or similar threat. Also, three immigrants mentioned that they had been threatened this way by their American spouses.

It was the common practice for the price of Green Card marriage to be paid in installments.[7] The first payment was delivered before or on the day of the marriage ceremony,[8] the last on the divorce day, and other payments were scattered in between. There was no fixed schedule as to when any future payments were to be delivered. It depended on the immigrant's needs to move to the next step of the process. Any time an immigrant needed to meet his/her American spouse, payment was to be made.[9] The exceptions were arrangements where the immigrant agreed to pay for the living expenses (such as rent, bills, or school tuition) of the American spouse. In that case, payments were made regularly, usually monthly. GCMF broker Naomi explained how she handled payments:

> [Y]ou will charge eight thousand ($8,000) total amount. You gonna charge four thousand ($4,000) upfront. Of that four thousand ($4,000) upfront the first [you] do, you gonna give the girl a thousand dollars ($1,000). So you gonna pocket three ($3,000) for yourself. You tell her "the rest of the money that's left over is going to be given from your spouse." The broker only deals on the initial payment because most brokers don't want the person to know how much money they are actually going to be given to begin the process with. Me, I'm a little different. I rather just say it because then it becomes an issue.[10]

HOW TO DECEIVE IMMIGRATION OFFICIALS

Getting married to a U.S. citizen is just the first step on the way to the permanent residency. The next step is submitting Form I-130, Petition for Alien Relative, and evidence of a bona fide marriage to U.S. Citizenship and Immigration Services (USCIS). Since the immigrant is already in the United States, this process is called Adjustment of Status. A bona fide marriage is one in which both spouses intend to establish a life together as husband and wife.[11] The burden of proof is on the couple to establish their bona fide marriage.

There are numerous documents that can be used to establish that spouses entered a genuine marriage. According to the Instructions for Form I-130, USCIS requires petitioners to submit one or more of the following types of documentation that may prove one has a bona fide marriage:

1. Documentation showing joint ownership of property.
2. A lease showing joint tenancy of a common residence, meaning you both live at the same address together.
3. Documentation showing that you and your spouse have combined your financial resources.
4. Birth certificates of children born to you and your spouse together;
5. Affidavits sworn to or affirmed by third parties having personal knowledge of the bona fides of the marital relationship. Each affidavit must contain the full name and address of the person making the affidavit; date and place of birth of the person making the affidavit; and complete information and details explaining how the person acquired his or her knowledge of your marriage.
6. Any other relevant documentation to establish that there is an ongoing marital union (USCIS, 2019a, p. 7).

Documentation showing joint ownership of property is a strong proof of bona fide marriage. However, with the mean income of the participants in the study being $1,056.7 per month for U.S. citizens and $2,470 per month for immigrants, their chances to own property are very low. Only one U.S. citizen, Rob, made an agreement with his wife to include him in a loan plan for her newly purchased vehicle. For Rob, it was a crucial point of their arrangement as his goal was to build credit history, to be able to buy a house in the future. For his immigrant wife, this joint loan would serve as a proof of joint ownership of the vehicle.

The data obtained showed that leases involving joint tenancy of a common residence were much easier to secure than the join ownership of property. Twenty-two interviewees had never lived together with their GCMF spouse. Five interviewees (four U.S. citizens and one immigrant) had some type of experiences living with their spouse. Three out of five created living "on and off" situations. They had some personal belongings in the residency they shared with the new spouse and sometimes stayed there overnight.[12] However, they spent half or more of their time in the residency where they lived before engaging in GCMF. Two U.S. citizens actually moved in with their new immigrant spouses with the intent to live together for approximately two years (until the immigrant spouse could receive a Green Card).

Despite the fact that the majority of study participants lived apart from their spouses, all 27 of them had leases showing joint tenancy of a common residence with their GCMF spouses. In 24 cases, the immigrants added the U.S. citizens to an already existing lease in the place where they actually resided. In two cases, the immigrant rented an apartment where the U.S. citizen spouse moved (in both cases from the homeless shelter) but despite single occupancy, both names were included on the lease. In one case, the immigrant moved in with his new wife.

Documentation showing spouses having combined financial resources was an unproblematic piece of evidence to produce. Twenty-five study participants stated they had at least one joint bank account with their spouse. In all cases, both spouses went to the bank together and opened the joint bank account. If they had a bank account before opening a joint one, they kept it open for their own use. With respect to their own personal bank accounts, none of the study participants added funds or gave access in any form to their sham marriage partner. Each of the interviewed immigrants and 12 U.S. citizens declared that since the Green Card marriage was *"not real,"* they would never trust their spouse with their money. Spouses did not keep savings or deposit their salaries into the joint bank account. Twenty-two study participants stated that they were being paid (U.S. citizens) or were paying (immigrants) for the GCMF using joint bank accounts. Instead of paying in cash, immigrants were depositing money into joint bank accounts from which withdrawals were made exclusively by citizen-spouses. The immigrants stated that this option was important for documenting how much money their citizen-spouse received.[13] Spouses also explained that since they did not live together (sometimes they lived in different cities), the joint bank account helped immigrants to send money quickly to their spouses if they requested it.[14] To summarize, a joint bank account did not represent combined financial resources. It was created only to deceive immigration officials in order to demonstrate the trust and economic unity existing within the new family.

Birth certificates of children born to the GCMF spouses in the study could not be shown to immigration officials because the individuals interviewed for this study did not have children with their spouses. Thirteen participating U.S. citizens and one immigrant had children with someone other than the GCMF spouse. Within this group, three female citizens got pregnant while being legally married to the immigrant spouse. In none of the cases did GCMF spouses adopt the spouse's child or legally share the custody of the child.

On the other hand, the study's participants were likely to include in the documentation supporting their I-130 application form (the "Petition for Alien Relative"), affidavits by third parties having personal knowledge of the bona fides of their marital relationship. Most of the time, the person signing an affidavit was a family member or best friend of the immigrant, less likely a family member or friend of the U.S. citizen.[15]

Spouses also produced additional documentation to support establishment of an ongoing marital union. Naomi, a marriage fraud broker, explained how she coaches her clients to produce necessary evidence:

Just a typical evidence that they really need to show they are together. You need to show you live together, share the same address, have bills together; you need to prove you are married. You just do simple things that real married people do. You get phones with each other names, get rent deal, get cable, get bills, get bank accounts, take pictures, get plenty of pictures, buy membership cards, like join a gym together. This pretty much all you gotta do. Oh. And file taxes together!

Most of the interviewees followed steps mentioned by Naomi. According to study participants, the most likely financial responsibility they shared was a phone line.[16] Twenty-two participants said they had a family plan for their cellphones, so both spouses' phones were on the same account. Twenty-one interviewees stated they had bills together with their GCMF spouse. The same way spouses added each other to the lease showing joint tenancy (as explained above), they added their spouse's name to the bills for residential services. Sixteen interviewees mentioned they had a joint electricity account, and nine mentioned a cable account. Nine participants shared a family health insurance plan with their GCMF spouse, and nine filed a joint tax return. Two participants shared a gym membership with their spouses, two shared a grocery store membership, and one had a shared credit card account with a $500 limit.

All interviewees produced pictures documenting their bona fide marriage. Kofi said:

"We took pictures; pictures of us . . . I mean the marriage [ceremony] where we've been and basically everything. I mean stuff we did together, like we went to restaurant, or for a walk, or sat in my home, that's what we did mostly–took pictures because a requirement is that you need a proof." Later he added *"Every time I meet her [wife] we take plenty of pictures. And we change clothes, so it looks like we met many times."*

Study participants explained how important it was to also include other people in the pictures, especially family members and friends to show that their marriage was socially recognized. Five interviewees mentioned inviting their spouse to family gatherings, Christmas celebrations, or birthday parties just to take pictures of the spouse being part of important events. Four participants, like Kofi, discussed changing clothes during the meeting with their spouse (changing also the date in their cameras) to take as many photos as possible in a short amount of time. Later, the pictures would be used to help to create the fictional story of a close relationship between spouses and the amount of family time they spent together.

It was essential that the pictures looked realistic and authentic, showing an emotional bond between the spouses. The study participants had to pretend to be in love when they had to. Of course, quite the opposite was true; the majority of the participants had no romantic or intimate relationship with their GCMF spouses. Only one interviewed immigrant and two U.S. citizens admitted to having sexual intercourse with their GCMF spouses. All three, had some experience of living together with their spouses. Frank, an immigrant, said he had sexual intercourse with his wife a couple of times but also highlighted that no romantic feelings were involved in this relationship. For Anna and Paula (U.S. citizens), the intercourse was a single incident and they both regretted their intimate involvement. Anna explained reasons for engaging in this sexual intercourse in the following words:

> *There is one time, that was like one month after marriage, happen to be his birthday. I think it was more or less of an action that came out of culmination of curiosity and alcohol put together. Because we were married, we were somehow living together, so there was always that "why not give it a shot and see what is there," and especially if you've been drinking there is more motivation to do some networking [pause] But it wasn't very fulfilling for either of us. But then, it can only be factual from my half.*

The remaining nine immigrants and 15 U.S. citizens strongly confirmed that there were no romantic feelings, romantic or intimate situations, or sexual intercourse between them and their GCMF spouses. Moreover, five immigrants and three U.S. citizens highlighted that they found their spouses unattractive and they would never consider a relationship with them outside of Green Card marriage. Tania explained:

> *Intimate with him? Are you serious? No way! Never, ever. He is . . . he is really not attractive. I mean, you have to see him. But no, not possible, even in million years.*

Additionally, posing for romantic pictures with spouses that some participants find unattractive was difficult, but as Jamal explained:

> *Game of pretense is a part of the deal. You gotta do it, and you gotta do it well, if you don't want to screw you both and get busted by immigration [USCIS].*

After the couples had submitted their I-130 forms along with other required documents, they needed to begin preparing for an in-person interview with USCIS officers. During these interviews, the bona fide nature of the marriage is tested. Twenty-five participants stated they prepared or were planning to prepare for an immigration interview together. Steven explained: "*You get [aaa] questions over the Internet . . . sample questions of course. And you try to go over those questions with her [wife]. And see if you get lucky.*" Francis recollected preparing for his interview in the following way:

> *What we pretty much ended up having to do, was to write each other's life stories, you know, then pull up some questions from internet, guiding questions and ask each other. We got to know each other between the time we got married and the time we applied for Green Card and were up to interview. We got to know each other like that. So, we pretty much structured it that way. Or I will say, I did structured it. So pretty much I told her my life story, she had to learn and then I asked her something about my life. [. . .] We ended up calling each other and asking questions: who is your mother, who is your brother, do you know this, do you know this about me? So, we ended up know a lot about each other before we walked in [for an interview].*

Most of the couples prepared in a similar way to Francis. Three interviewees said they made pictures of the apartment they lived in (where both spouses claim to officially live together) to help their spouse memorize details about their apartment/house. Moreover, some participants got help from their marriage broker or even a lawyer. Two brokers, Naomi and Steven, used mock interviews to help their clients prepare. Anna said the lawyer set up a conference call for her and her husband and practiced how to answer interview questions with them.

ROLE OF THE MARRIAGE FRAUD BROKER AND OTHERS AIDING, ABETTING, AND ACTING AS AN ACCESSORY TO GREEN CARD MARRIAGE FRAUD

Based on its nature, the "cash-for-vows" type of fraud marriage always involves at least two offenders—spouses who enter a marriage to evade the immigration laws of the United States. Depending on the individual situation of the immigrant, such as current immigration status, personal characteristics, background, and understanding of legal procedures, some couples may need more help from third parties than others to successfully conduct a fraud marriage—that is to obtain a Green Card for an immigrant spouse—without raising suspicions of USCIS officers. People who aid, abet, and act as an accessory to Green Card marriages bond together forming unofficial groups in order to increase the number of customers they serve, the financial gain that comes with it, and the approval rate of their customers for obtaining their goal of permanent residency. These various participants form a type of "working group," having both a set of operating principles and an observable structure.

GCMF is not a single illegal act but a series of fraudulent activities that create an illusion of the happy conjugal life of the Green Card applicant and the contracted American citizen-spouse. The illusion must be good enough to deceive USCIS officers trained in fraud detection. Therefore, the clearly focused and organized efforts of a range of people are needed for the immigrant to achieve the goal of permanent residency.

Often, GCMFs are kept in secret from family and friends by both the immigrants and their American spouses. In this study, the state in which the participants were married did not require that witnesses be present at the marriage ceremony. Nevertheless, the number of people present during wedding ceremonies ranged from two to 10 people; on average four people including the spouses.[17] The majority of the wives-to-be invited for the ceremony their best female friend or a sister, while the husbands-to-be invited his best male friend or a brother. In most cases, those who attended the wedding ceremony were the only people informed that the parties had married. Four interviewees (three U.S. citizens and one immigrant) stated that their family[18] was aware of the situation; out of those, only three introduced the spouse to their family or was introduced by the spouse to the in-laws.

THE ELEMENTS OF ORGANIZED CRIME

The definition of organized crime is the object of continuing controversy. It is usually conceptualized not as a specific crime, but rather as a large number of illegal activities committed by individuals working in a structured organization. Hagan (2006) highlighted four of the most frequently identified traits used to define organized crime:

- Represented a continuing, organized hierarchy.
- Profiteering from illegal activities.
- Using violence and threats.
- Represented corruption and immunity.

The FBI defines organized crime as:

Any group having some manner of a formalized structure and whose primary objective is to obtain money through illegal activities. Such groups maintain their position through the use of actual or threatened violence, corrupt public officials, graft, or extortion, and generally have a significant impact on the people in their locales, region, or the country as a whole. (FBI, n.d., _Organized Crime Glossary_)

This definition is broad and extends beyond what many may consider to be traditional organized crime activities.

There is currently no statutory definition of organized crime. However, the *Racketeer Influenced and Corrupt Organizations Act* (RICO) defines organized crime in terms of an "enterprise" and a "pattern of racketeering activity."[19] RICO allows for the prosecution of anyone who participates or conspires to participate in a criminal enterprise/organization through two acts of racketeering activity within a 10-year period. The predicate offenses for racketeering include various state and federal crimes listed in the U.S. Code (18 U.S. Code § 1961) such as murder, kidnapping, gambling, arson, robbery, bribery, extortion, acts relating to fraud in foreign labor, procurement of citizenship or nationalization unlawfully, reproduction or sale of naturalization or citizenship papers, obstruction of justice or criminal investigation, fraud and misuse of visas, permits, and other documents, but also any act which is indictable under the *Immigration and Nationality Act* (INA), relating to bringing in and harboring certain aliens, or relating to aiding or assisting certain aliens to enter the United States, if such act was committed for the purpose of financial gain.[20]

Organized crime exists as a diverse, multidimensional phenomenon and can involve many different types of offenses. GCMF is not a classic example of organized crime, but it meets most of the conditions specified above.

While GCMF is not specified on the list of acts included in the definition of "racketeering activity" in 18 U.S. Code § 1961, several sections are linked to it. For example, section 1425 refers to the procurement of citizenship or nationalization unlawfully, as well as any act which is indictable under the INA; and section 277 refers to aiding or assisting certain aliens to enter the United States.

Moreover, GCMF has a recognizable organizational structure. Each of the marriage fraud brokers in the author's study explained how they cooperated with other people in order to perform their job. They knew other marriage fraud brokers with whom they often collaborated. During Naomi's interview, she made it clear that Elizabeth is working for her. Naomi had been in the GCMF business for 15 years, but her position on the GCMF market was strong because she was brought to the business by her mother who had worked as a marriage fraud broker for over 40 years. She explained her introduction to the GCMF business in the following words:

> *I started looking for girls when I was sixteen (16). Started, on my birthday she [mother] used to give me . . . those [customers] used to be my presents, on my birthdays. Well, let's say two (2) immigrants to marry would be my birthday presents. So, then I would go do two (2) and if I do those two (2) good, each one*

of those immigrants gave me three (3) immigrants. So, then I started learning
how to do it by myself.

Naomi's mother was still working as a marriage fraud broker at the time
of the interview, but Naomi rarely collaborated with her. Naomi helped her
mother only when she had a problem finding a proper U.S. citizen spouse for a
new immigrant customer. According to Naomi, her business was doing better
than her mother's because she was more caring about her customers. She said:

I started learning how to do it with my mom. But that's why my rules changed
from my mom's rules. Because I got the chance to see where it goes right and
where it goes wrong. And what is the problem. You get what I mean? As I
learned that I was able to polish my rules.

Naomi also reported that her business was more successful than her
mother's. When asked how many couples she connected for the purpose of
GCMF, her answer was *"thousands."*[21] At the time of the interview, she was
finalizing at least two or three marriages per week. However, she highlighted
that during some special times, such as during a presidential campaign, just
before the elections, and during tax season she has gotten *"tremendously*
more" customers. She believed that every happy customer brings her [on
average] three other customers. Therefore, it was important to her to develop
good customer service skills.

When an immigrant is seeking to engage in GCMF and contacts Naomi,
she knows that she must act fast, as immigrants are eager to learn if she has
a potential spouse for them. In order to find willing citizen spouses, Naomi
has recruited other women to help find them.[22] These women usually tried to
recruit from a circle of their own acquaintances as well as the acquaintances
of their acquaintances. However, when such searches proved difficult, the
effort was widened to include strangers. This could involve approaching
people in various waiting lines or standing outside of welfare offices. Naomi
and other marriage fraud brokers usually paid a fee of $500 to the persons
finding a U.S. citizen ready to enter GCMF. When Naomi got more customers than she could handle, she sent some of them to Elizabeth, as collaboration between marriage fraud brokers was commonplace. They exchanged
customers, sometimes shared the services of the women helping to find
potential U.S. citizen spouses, and exchanged experiences about deceiving
immigration officials.

Marriage fraud brokers also collaborated with justices of the peace.[23] Such
corruption seems to come directly out of the playbook of organized crime
activities. Naomi admitted to collaboration with three justices of the peace on
the regular basis. She also used services of justices of the peace in other states

when she assisted clients who resided and wanted to get married outside of Massachusetts. Naomi stated that her clients are successful in getting their Green Cards because she has access to inside information and collaborates with people working in the USCIS,[24] justices of the peace, and immigration attorneys. Through her connections, she had gained the knowledge to successfully lead her customers through the immigration process. She said:

> *As long as you stick to my rules we are ok. Because we gonna do all the paperwork they need, we gonna make sure we will put you with the lawyer, and I mean, hell, when you go with me I got couple of people that work there [USCIS] too. I got to put my ass to work with immigration. So you know, I was scheduled to know when things will change, to get a fax about something different. You know. So it's all about who you get to know.*

Naomi shared inside information with those marriage fraud brokers with whom she had developed a trusting relationship. Elizabeth also indicated that she knew a justice of the peace familiar with GCMF to whom she was sending her customers. She had also collaborated with an immigration attorney. However, she did not mention personally knowing or collaborating with any USCIS officers. Elizabeth admitted that she had obtained most of her information from Naomi. The third interviewed marriage fraud broker, Steven, did not mention knowing or collaborating with USCIS officers nor justices of peace. But he admitted to knowing immigration attorneys who assisted with GCMF.

The next characteristic often required when classifying a criminal activity as an organized crime is that offenders must profit from their criminal activity. Immigrants had different motives to engage in GCMF, including freedom of movement; opportunity to get legal employment, and to enroll in school, etc.[25] U.S. citizens and marriage fraud brokers engaged in GCMF mainly for financial gain. U.S. citizens received between three thousand ($3,000) and eleven thousand dollars ($11,000) per marriage.[26]

Marriage fraud brokers are career offenders who consider GCMF as their business. According to Treverton et al. (2009), organized crime groups act to generate profits: "In this sense, these groups are like business enterprises: They make rational choices about what "business" activities they engage in, whom they partner with, and how they manage their product lines and respond to market demands" (p.12). Marriage fraud brokers treat their criminal activity as a business and focus on increasing profits while decreasing risks involved.

One apparent criterion of organized crime that GCMF does not generally satisfy concerns the use of violence to achieve a criminal goal.[27] However, GCMF is perceived as a "threat to U.S. national security, financial institutions, and the integrity of the immigration system" (ICE, 2014b, p. 2). Moreover, the previously presented criteria are more fundamental to distinguishing the phenomenon of organized crime from other criminal activities. Therefore, GCMF can potentially be treated as organized crime.

NOTES

1. Including those that were described by U.S. citizens who engaged in Green Card marriage more than once.

2. Thirteen interviewees described their activities after the marriage ceremony, but three people were not asked or did not provide information to answer this question.

3. Six out of seven and eight out of 10 U.S. citizens brought a sibling or a best friend to the meeting. Two citizens considered the marriage fraud broker to be their close friend and did not need additional support. One immigrant came to the meeting by himself.

4. Average price was calculated based on estimates given by 25 interviewees. One immigrant stated that he/she doesn't want to reveal the price paid for the marriage. One U.S. citizen stated that his/her spouse was paying for his/her living expenses (rent, bills, grocery, etc.) and he/she was not able to estimate the price his/her spouse paid for the marriage.

5. Total price includes amount paid directly to the American spouse as well as amount paid to the marriage fraud broker for his/her service, if broker was involved. It is impossible to separate the amount going to the American spouse from the amount going to the broker as participants are not aware how much money was divided between such persons. Marriage fraud brokers may try to confuse participants during the initial part of the process. It is important to note that initial meetings are organized by the broker, and the broker participates in them, and contact between GCMF participants is controlled by the broker. This situation is sustained until the broker receives all the money. Only after that the broker steps out of the transaction are the spouses more likely to communicate with each other.

6. Divorcing the immigrant spouse and, as a petitioner, subsequently withdrawing a Petition for Alien Relative.

7. Description of the installment payments is based on the information given by all three marriage fraud brokers and 16 U.S. citizens and nine immigrants. One U.S. citizen and one immigrant were not aware of how the payments were handled because their relatives dealt with it.

8. If a marriage fraud broker is involved, the first payment was the marriage day. Those who engaged in Green Card marriage without the help of a broker usually paid or received a payment on the day of the marriage.

9. Spouses must meet multiple times in order to produce evidence of living together—that includes setting up a joint bank account, creating history of the relationship by taking pictures from various events, preparing for immigration interview, interview itself, and more.

10. Further, Naomi explained what she meant by "issue." She described situations when immigrants were trying to figure out how much the broker got paid for his/her service and how much money the immigrant actually gave to the broker with the intention that this money will be delivered by the broker to his/her American spouse. When the American spouse learned that the immigrant gave more money for him/her to the broker, the American demanded their share. The process of passing money was intentionally made confusing and somehow secretive. Often, both spouses had a hard time understanding how the money were distributed. Sometimes, these kinds of situations caused arguments that escalated to the point where both sides did not want to participate in the marriage anymore and Naomi had to find another U.S. citizen to finish the transaction.

11. "Husband and husband" and "wife and wife" is currently also acceptable based on the Supreme Court decisions. In *United States v. Windsor* (2013) the U.S. Supreme Court declared Section 3 of *The Defense of Marriage Act* unconstitutional under the Due Process Clause of the Fifth Amendment. *Obergefell v. Hodges* (2015) struck down the act's provisions disallowing same-sex marriages to be performed under federal jurisdiction. Therefore, same-sex marriages are acceptable for U.S. immigration purposes, as long as they are legally valid in the state or country where they were entered into.

12. All three interviewees explained they came to the apartment/house they shared with the spouse between once a week to a few times a week, hoping neighbors would see them in order to create an impression that they lived there permanently.

13. Four immigrants explained that keeping track of all money given to the spouse is crucial as spouses are sometimes untruthful about how much money they received. In some cases (three immigrants), citizen spouses complained to marriage brokers who arranged their marriages that they did not get the amount of money they were promised, hoping that the marriage broker would pressure the immigrant spouse for more payments.

14. Since both spouses have ATM cards, an immigrant-spouse can deposit money and the citizen-spouse can easily withdraw this money in just a few minutes.

15. This researcher did not ask questions regarding who signed the affidavit. Only five immigrants, four citizens and one marriage fraud broker mentioned it when answering questions about the types of documents that spouses must produce for USCIS as evidence supporting their Form I-130, Petition for Alien Relative. However, marriage brokers coach their clients to include it and consider it "easy to obtain evidence."

16. This was a fictional responsibility since, in reality, only the immigrants are paying the bills.

17. Exact mathematical average is 4.4; without including the justice of the peace.

18. By informed family it is understood that a minimum of two family members were aware that the interviewee was involved in GCMF.

19. 18 U.S.C. § 1961 et seq. This is the centerpiece of the *Organized Crime Control Act* of 1970 (P.L. 91-452). RICO is one of the dominant tools used in organized crime prosecutions.

20. See Appendix 2 for ca omplete list of racketeering acts identified in 18 U.S. Code § 1961.

21. Author suspects this an overstatement but more accurate determination of the actual number of Naomi's clients is impossible at this time. Three other interviewees who know Naomi, when asked about possible number of her customers, said she had "hundreds," "a lot," and "crazy number."

22. First, she said few, but in the follow-up question she clarified that she has about fifteen (15) to twenty (20) girls that she is constantly using.

23. An attempt was made to interview two justices of the peace who engage in GCMF. They did not agree to participate in the study. However, the fact that contact was established and they unofficially confirmed that they collaborate with a marriage fraud broker (Naomi) is very important information that should be further explored in future research.

24. Naomi did not want to specify what type of USCIS officers she knows or what exactly the collaboration with them looks like. The only detail that was shared during the interview is that she is being immediately informed if new questions are being asked during the immigration interview (there are standard questions that interviewers use but from time to time they add something new to the list to surprise interviewees), so she has time to warn her customers who are preparing for the interview.

25. More detailed information was already presented in the subchapter Motivations for Engaging in GCMF.

26. More detailed information was already presented in the subchapter Marriage Price Negotiations.

27. In "cash-for-vows" type of GCMF, the violence or threat of violence is very rare. However, it is worth mentioning that in other types of GCMF such as "mail order bride arrangements," "family arranged marriages," and "heartbreakers" violence and threat of violence are not rare. This topic should be explored in future research.

Chapter Nine

Explanations

This chapter applies two criminological theories to help explain the reasons for Green Card marriage fraud (GCMF). This discussion has been purposely delayed until now in order to present the informed results of a grounded theory approach (Strauss and Corbin, 1998; Lowdermilk and Brunache, 2013) as presented in this subchapter. The theories discussed include Sykes and Matza's (1957) neutralization theory and Cornish and Clarke's (1987) rational choice theory to understand rationalizations and choices of those engaged in GCMF. In this study both theories emerged to partially explain the GCMF phenomenon and to clarify the behaviors of those engaged in it. Grounded theory is a method of research that seeks to develop or construct new theories based on collected data. The completed research suggests that the basic premises of neutralization theory and rational choice theory are useful to explain GCMF. Discussion first centers on the techniques of neutralization in order to explain participation in GCMF by immigrants, U.S. citizens, and marriage brokers.

NEUTRALIZATION THEORY

The neutralization theory of Sykes and Matza (1957) posits that delinquent individuals continually attempt to reintegrate with society by mentally asserting that their deviant behavior is actually normative, in essence, acceptable or "excusable." Sykes and Matza propose five following excuses, also called techniques of neutralization:

1. Denial of Responsibility: reflects individuals' beliefs that delinquent behavior was accidental or due to forces beyond their control. They see themselves as victims of circumstances beyond their control.
2. Denial of Injury: centers on the injury or harm involved in the delinquent act. Individuals may think that their actions are tolerable because they did not cause any harm or damage.
3. Denial of Victim: individuals may accept that injuries happened, but argue for their rightfulness considering the circumstances. The injury is not really an injury but rather deserved punishment or retaliation.
4. Condemning the Condemners: individuals may shift the focus of attention from their own deviant acts to the motives and behavior of those who disapprove of their behaviors.
5. Appeal to Higher Loyalties: individuals believe that his or her offense was for the greater good; they sacrificed the demands of the larger society for the demands of the smaller social group to which they belong, like a group of friends or a gang (Sykes and Matza, 1957).

By using one or more of these techniques, the individuals can convince themselves that what they are doing is acceptable behavior regardless of what societal norms dictate.

Research has shown that techniques of neutralization have been utilized by offenders for a variety of crimes and offenses. To list a few: rapists (Scully and Marolla, 1984); white-collar criminals (Benson, 1985; Vieraitis et al, 2012); violent criminals (Byers and Crider, 2002; Pogrebin et al., 2006; Presser, 2004); property criminals (Copes, 2003; Cromwell and Thurman, 2003); drug criminals (Peretti-Watel, 2003; Priest and McGrath, 1970); digital pirates (Morris and Higgins, 2009); cyclists using performance-enhancing drugs (Sefiha, 2012); and cyber-criminals (Holt and Copes, 2010; Moore and McMullan, 2009; Marcum et al., 2011). Some studies even examined the use of neutralization techniques by victims of crime (Ferraro and Johnson, 1983; Higginson, 1999).

Significantly, Ryo (2015) used the neutralization framework to study immigration noncompliance. Her goal was to find what unlawfully present people think about their own presence in the United States and how unauthorized border crossing impacts their view of themselves as law-abiding. She examined unauthorized immigrants and their relationship to the law from a novel perspective. The only visible method that can be used to get good quality data is qualitative interview. Ryo organized ten group interviews with 64 current and prospective unauthorized immigrants from Latin America. She chose group interviews over individual interviews for a number of reasons but mainly because group interactions and dynamics were "helpful in teasing out the law related views of the immigrants" (p. 644). Ryo asked them about their reasons to migrate to the United States and why they continued to work and reside in the United States in violation of immigration law, experiences with border crossing, and their attitudes toward the U.S. government, U.S. citizens, and U.S. immigration law.

Ryo (2015) concluded that immigrants view themselves as moral, law-abiding individuals. Many of them even respect "the purported sanctity of national borders and a belief that sovereign nations have a fundamental prerogative to control their borders" (Ryo, 2015, p. 648). However, in order to justify their decisions regarding unauthorized migration, immigrants most likely first used denial of responsibility and appeals to higher loyalties techniques, and later denial of injury and condemnation of condemners' techniques. For the immigrants, denials of responsibility and appeals to higher loyalties techniques are closely interwoven. Denial of responsibility was expressed by claims that their actions were due to forces beyond their control or accidental. Individuals highlighted personal blamelessness for their situation. The situation in their countries of origin was so bad that migration was the only option for them. An appeal to higher loyalties technique usually involved immigrants' duty to care for their families. They often considered family to be the most important value, and unmet family needs were a strong push to cross the border illegally.

The denial of injury technique emerged from Ryo's interviews in response to a line of questioning about whether unauthorized immigrants might be displacing native workers in the United States. Interviewees drew attention to the "legal" and "honorable" nature of the work in which they engaged. In their opinion, Americans cannot claim injury (lowering wages and taking away jobs from citizens) because they would never agree to work low-wage and low-status jobs that immigrants want to do. Moreover, immigrants drew a distinction between immigration law and other laws. What Ryo saw in this was a distinction between actions that are deemed *mala in se* (actions wrong in themselves such as murder or rape) and actions that are deemed *mala prohibita* (actions proclaimed by the government to be wrong)—a distinction known from Anglo-American law. Her interviewees explained that immigration law is different from other laws. They crossed the border in violation of immigration law forced by necessity, but they did not think it made them criminals. Moreover, in their opinion, necessity would not justify other forms of legal noncompliance. Disobeying immigration law was of a different moral caliber than committing unrelated crimes.

Finally, immigrants also used the condemnation of the condemners' technique. They shifted the focus of attention from their actions to the motivations or behaviors of those who disapprove of their behavior. Ryo's interviewees pointed to three fundamentally unfair aspects of the U.S. immigration system: (1) class bias or the privileging of the wealthy (poor people are excluded from getting visas); (2) racial bias (immigrants from Latin America are at a significant disadvantage within the U.S. immigration system); and (3) hypocrisy and arbitrariness apparent in the system. The U.S. economy has come to depend heavily on the labor of unauthorized immigrants and this has influenced the creation of immigration system privileges for certain national-origin groups, such as an exemption from deportation granted to Salvadorans.[1]

Ryo's (2015) findings are in accord with findings in the current study. Similar to the Ryo study, the immigrants in the present study viewed themselves as moral, law-abiding individuals, and saw GCMF as a one-time, justifiable event that does not make them criminals. When asked about their criminal history, all ten interviewed immigrants stated that they had never been involved in any other criminal activity, other than GCMF. To present some support for their statements, three of them highlighted that to obtain a visa to the United States, one has to pass stringent background checks. All interviewed immigrants understood that GCMF is a crime and tried to justify their decision regarding participation in this illegal activity. They used techniques of neutralization to justify their engagement in GCMF in the same order as techniques used to justify decisions regarding unauthorized migration in the population studied by Ryo (2015). Both groups were most likely to use the denial of responsibility, appeal to higher loyalties, denial of injury, and condemnation of condemners' techniques.

Denial of responsibility reflects individuals' beliefs that delinquent behavior is accidental or due to forces beyond their control. They see themselves as victims of circumstances beyond their control (Sykes and Matza, 1957). All interviewed immigrants were strongly convinced that they were left with no other choice to legalize their permanent status in the United States, and therefore should not be blamed for their actions. Specifically, when asked about the reasons behind the decision to get involved in GCMF, eight immigrants used the exact words *"that was the only way"* or *"the only option."*[2] Moreover, they explained that having no legal status in the U.S. forced them into participation in criminal activities on a daily basis; for example, they had to use fraudulent documents or use someone else's documents in order to obtain employment or they were forced to drive without a driver's license since lack of legal status makes it impossible to apply for a license. Kofi explained his reasons to engage in GCMF:

> [when you finally obtain a Green Card] *you feel like you are normal human being. You act right. If police stop you, you show him that you also legal. You don't have to act like you are trying to hide; you tryin' hide from people or tryin'*

do anything illegal. You wanna do everything straight. The only way to get access to this country is through the marriage, that's the only thing . . . or you've been adopted or something. That's the only way.

The appeal to higher loyalties technique, involving a belief that crime was committed for the greater good, was used by eight immigrants. Seven out of this group claimed that they took care of their families in their countries of origin. This explanation also parallels with explanation provided by immigrants interviewed by Ryo (2015). Both groups highlight the disadvantaged situation of people living in their countries. Family was very important to them, thus the duty to financially support the family was taken as a necessity. According to Natalie:

[GCMF] No other option that was the only option. I don't regret it because I just try to find a better life, so I can help my family. That is my main goal.

The third technique, denial of injury, is based on the belief that the offender's illegal actions are tolerable because they did not cause any harm or damage. Three interviewed immigrants stated that not only did no one get hurt during the process of GCMF, but they improved the situation of their American spouses. Kofi said:

The person that they [marriage brokers] bring for you is not somebody who is perfect. They bring somebody like [aaa] . . . somebody from the hood, who needs help already, who need money. Somebody who has no job. [. . .] And I took care of her; help her to pay bills. [. . .] She wouldn't be where she is now without me.

Another immigrant, Miguel, expressed a similar sentiment. He was convinced that without his financial support his American wife would have ended up in a shelter. All three quoted immigrants believe that they saved their spouses from severe consequences of poverty. Therefore, they not only saw their criminal activity as victimless but almost as heroic. In a similar way, immigrants interviewed by Ryo (2015) explained that without their support, that is support of low-wage and low-status laborers, the U.S. economy would experience a great loss. In both cases, immigrants saw themselves as "saviors" rather than criminals.

The fourth and last technique used by interviewed immigrants is "condemnation of the condemners." This neutralization technique involves shifting the focus of attention from one's own deviant acts to the motives and behavior of those who disapprove of his/her behaviors (Sykes and Matza, 1957). Freud referred to this concept as "projection." This mechanism can be seen as defensive if perceiving the threatening trait in others helps the individual to avoid (to some extent) recognizing it in himself or herself (Freud, 1915). As was described before, immigrants interviewed by Ryo (2015) considered the U.S. immigration system as unfair and biased. In this research, two interviewees also stated that U.S. immigration system was unfair. Both referred to the lack of fair educational opportunities and complained that tuition and fees for international students were so high as to make it impossible to enroll in college. These immigrants are already college educated in their countries of origin, so they saw education as a necessity. Immigrants are at a significant disadvantage within the U.S. educational system, and therefore feel it is justifiable to engage in GCMF in order to fight such inequality. Moreover, as mentioned, eight immigrants considered GCMF "*the only way*" to legalize their stay in the United States. The fact that they were stripped from other options to legalize their stay was seen as unjust. Therefore, they neutralized responsibility for engaging in GCMF by shifting the focus of attention from their criminal actions to "unfair" immigration law. Jan (immigrant from Poland) said:

I wanted study in the good university and pay the same money like American people because it was not fair for me that international students have to pay twice, they cannot work so they can't make money and cannot apply for any financial aid. Why system is like that? I don't understand this. But still, I wanted to finish study, so I get better possibilities here or in my country. But I knew that I was not able to pay for the first semester and I knew that if I don't wanna pay, I'm gonna stay . . . become overstayed [overstay F-1 visa]. So it means [if I leave] that I couldn't go back to the U.S. again. So, I wanted to have a Green Card or citizenship to be able to travel to the U.S. as much as I want. Not be trapped. That's why I did all this marriage thing [Green Card marriage fraud], That's the only option they [government] have left for us.

This research shows techniques of neutralization have been utilized by those participating in GCMF. Each group of interviewees, immigrants, U.S. citizens, and marriage brokers used different techniques of neutralization.

Moore and McMullan (2009) examined rationalizations used by digital pirates. They found denial of injury being the most commonly encountered technique. Based on characteristics of this group of offenders and the nature of the nonviolent crime they committed, comparisons can be made to U.S. citizens engaging in GCMF. American-spouses, similar to digital pirates, may be likely to use the "denial of injury" technique thinking there was no harm involved in their fraud marriage. Digital pirates tend to think their act will ultimately benefit the musician. U.S. citizens may feel that they help immigrants to fix their problems. Other researchers have also found similar results involving property crime (Hollinger, 1991; Copes, 2003).

Naomi also felt the system was unfair to her husband, an immigrant from Ghana, and that was one of the most important reasons why she decided to engage in GCMF. She explained:

> *I don't agree with the system. At that time person I married was going to school and his visa had ended. He just wanted to stay and finish up his studies and become a doctor. And they weren't to be able to extend the visa. [. . .] And he already was a medical doctor in Africa. He was medical down there, working in hospital. When he came here, he meant nothing! So, he had to go to school and do that all over again. All medical school. And he was doing very well. But when it [visa] started to expire out, he needed someone to help him stay. And I felt I want to help him out because he deserved it.*

Only two U.S. citizens felt some regret or guilt for their involvement in GCMF. Paula said she would not get involved in GCMF again because it was not worth it. Anita felt that she helped a wrong person—someone who did not deserve to be helped. The remaining 15 Americans said they did not regret their marriage with immigrants. U.S. citizens are most likely to first use "denial of injury," next "condemnation of condemners," then "denial of responsibility," and lastly "appeal to higher loyalties" techniques to neutralize their wrongdoing. All U.S. citizens stated that their action did not cause any harm or damage. When asked specifically if they saw the U.S. immigration system or government as a victim, their answer was still negative. Three citizens pointed out that their financial situation significantly improved after participation in GCMF, which limited the amount of financial assistance they need from the government. Lori said that she and her children did not have to stay in the shelter anymore, so *"the government should be happy."* David made the same point, highlighting the fact that GCMF helped him fight homelessness.

Thirteen U.S. citizens also used the "condemnation of the condemners" technique. Five of them, when asked if they saw the U.S. immigration system or government as a victim of GCMF, focused their answer on the U.S. government. Interviewees said government was responsible for their bad financial situation.[3] This was asserted as being due to various reasons, such as: lack of sufficient financial assistance, lack of job opportunities, expensive childcare system, and deficiency of proper housing options.[4] In addition, the participating U.S. citizens who were seeking to broaden their opportunities to improve their financial situation, blamed politicians and lawmakers for creating the situations where GCMF becomes an appealing option. Another four U.S. citizens blame the U.S. immigration system for being unfair toward immigrants. They understood the limitations that immigrants face based on the lack of their legal status in the United States and considered those limitations unjust. Their participation in GCMF was a response to compensate for this unfairness. Also, four U.S. citizens blamed both, the government and the U.S. immigration system. Juana explained why she decided to help a Turkish immigrant by getting married to him for immigration purposes:

> *I have a huge heart. So what it is, I knew legal consequences [of GCMF], but I thought about it as of this person is not allowed to study, this person is not allowed to live the normal American life that everybody just take for granted, we [American immigration system] screwed him. So I decided to help him. Because I know . . . I just know how it is, when the system screws you.*

Fifteen U.S. citizens stated that the main reason why they decided to participate in GCMF was financial benefits. All 15 highlighted their difficult economic situation. Eight U.S. citizens considered GCMF their only option to survive. They blamed forces beyond their control, government, and other factors (e.g., their family, friends, or fate) for their financial standing. Since they believed that they were victims of circumstances beyond their control, they considered their participation in GCMF to be justified, negating or neutralizing the guilt that comes with involvement in a fraudulent marriage with an immigrant.

Moreover, U.S. citizens utilized the appeals to higher loyalties technique. For 12 interviewed U.S. citizens, the possibility to help someone (future spouse) to better their life was one of the crucial push factors in deciding to marry an immigrant. For three out of those 12, this was the most important reason. As explained above, many citizens feel victimized by the existing system. Therefore, they understand the unique situation of individuals looking to engage in GCMF and empathize with them. Despite the financial gain, the fact that reasons for engaging in GCMF are somehow altruistic let participants neutralize potential guilt.

McCrory (2006) observed a federal court case in Alexandria, Virginia, involving a marriage fraud scheme. His report included a profile of a marriage fraud broker who used one of the techniques of neutralization to justify his criminal activity. Samuel Acquah was an immigrant from Ghana who had earned masters and law degrees from George Mason University. Prior to his arrest, he worked in the chemical engineering section of the U.S. Patent and Trademark Office in Alexandria with an annual salary of $112,000. He referred to his GCMF activity as "the program" to help fellow Ghanaian immigrants to stay in the United States legally. He also admitted to collecting an estimated $200,000. His statement appears to relate to the techniques of neutralization involving "denial of injury" and "appeal to higher loyalties."

In an effort to point out Acquah's false philanthropic rationale for his actions, U.S. District Court Judge T. S. Ellis III showed the felon, Samuel Acquah, a picture of his $775,000 house in Bowie, and said: "*That's a mansion you built.* . . . *You did this for greed. You didn't do it to help anyone. So get that notion out of your head.*" Adding that, "*Sham marriages, the number that you engaged in, the scheme that you engaged in, do serious injury to the proper administration of our immigration system.*" The above case depicts a use of two techniques of neutralization: denial of injury and appeal to higher loyalties.

Marriage fraud brokers were most likely to use condemnation of the condemner's technique, followed by the appeal to higher loyalties, and then the denial of injury techniques. All three interviewed brokers condemned the U.S. immigration system as well as the public assistance system. They highlighted that current policies are unfair for immigrants, limiting their employment and educational opportunities. On the other hand, in the eyes of brokers, certain groups of U.S. citizens (such as minorities or low-income people) were highly disadvantaged as well. Elizabeth said, "*the law only works for certain people; only benefits certain people.*" Therefore, they felt that by navigating couples through the GCMF process they helped them to get better. All brokers provided examples of U.S. citizens (their clients) whose living conditions were positively impacted as a result of participation in the GCMF. Naomi shared stories of a few single mothers who, by the time of invitation to participate in the GCMF, lived in a homeless shelter. Money obtained from a GCMF transaction and, often, help of immigrant spouse resulted in them leaving the shelter and moving into a rented apartment. Naomi highlighted that single mothers living in a homeless shelters are easy to convince to participate in a marriage fraud. She even mentioned that at some point all girls living in a particular shelter were her customers at the same time. Naomi was proud that some of these girls were able to turn their lives around because of the opportunity (as she thought of GCMF) that she provided. Improving lives of American spouses was an indirect component of GCMF transactions. Immigrants were interested in presenting to USCIS officials evidence of being a part of a happy and healthy family unit. Therefore, helping a U.S. citizen spouse to improve his/her overall living situation was embedded in the process.

Elizabeth and Naomi put more emphasis on issues faced by Americans, as they are Americans themselves. Both are females, racial minorities, and raised in low-income households. Therefore, they shared many characteristics with U.S. citizens engaging in GCMF. Steven, as an immigrant, shared many characteristics with immigrants participating in GCMF, so he empathized with them. When asked why he worked as a marriage fraud broker, besides financial gain, he said: "*I want to help my fellow Nigerians, and students.*" All brokers wanted to help those who were like them. They focused their attention on those whose struggles they understood from their own experience. By helping those who are disadvantaged, brokers neutralize their own potential guilt.

Finally, two brokers (Elizabeth and Naomi) expressed the belief that their work as marriage fraud brokers caused no harm to anyone. Elizabeth emphasized that she does not regard her work as criminal. She was convinced that immigrants would marry someone for a Green Card anyway, and all she does is to make the process faster and safer. Elizabeth understood the legal consequences of her actions, but she felt they were unfair. Naomi explained that everything she did was safe for participants; she did not put people at risk. Neither of these informants seemed to understand the complex consequences of GCMF for the country.

RATIONAL CHOICE THEORY

Rational choice theory may also serve as a partial explanation for some of the dynamics in the process of GCMF. All three interviewed groups acted in a rational way when getting involved in GCMF to maximize their net benefits. There were monetary and nonmonetary benefits that played a role in the process.

When deciding to engage in GCMF, immigrants took into consideration the sum of utilities over several dimensions like wealth, social status, safety, family well-being, comfort, autonomy, affiliation, and morality. Nine immigrants, directly or indirectly, referred to the improvement of their socioeconomic situation as a motivation to engage in GCMF. They expected that GCMF would result in a future financial gain, mainly through access to a broader range of employment opportunities that are inaccessible for unauthorized foreigners. Moreover, easier access to education was likely to improve quantity and quality of employment opportunities. Immigrants also hoped that permanent residency would greatly increase their perceived safety level by removing the possibility of deportation.[5] This, in turn, would improve their sense of belonging to their communities and expand social interactions. Finally, legal status was associated with the possibility of obtaining health insurance and receiving medical help if needed.

However, there were also costs of GCMF that immigrants had to take into consideration. These costs include primarily risk of imprisonment, fines, and deportation. In order to engage in a cost-benefit analysis, one must be aware of these costs. The majority of interviewed immigrants had inaccurate knowledge regarding potential consequences of fraud marriage.[6] Only three immigrants stated that they were aware of potential penalties, and only one expected a penalty similar to that provided by law. Others diminished probable consequences or said they did not know what the risks involved were. Despite their lack of factual knowledge, all interviewed immigrants were aware that they had engaged in criminal behavior and were afraid of being caught. However, their main fear was deportation and lack of future opportunity to return to the United States, not imprisonment or fines. Therefore, rational choice explanation can be applied to the process of deciding to engage in GCMF, as all immigrants clearly explained expected benefits of GCMF and potential risks (even if those risks were diminished or inaccurate, they were understood as serious consequences of criminal behavior).

Rational choice explanation can be applied also to the behavior of U.S. citizens. Fifteen of them stated that the main reason why they decided to participate in GCMF was financial gain. Americans were more explicit than immigrants regarding their financial needs. They highlighted their low income[7] and family needs. Thirteen of them had children (five out of 12 had three children or more), and one was in advanced pregnancy. However, for a majority (12), the opportunity to help someone was also an incentive. Trice presented reasons to engage in GCMF that is representative of the reasoning of the majority of the interviewed citizens. She said:

> *Why I married him? Because he needed help and I needed help at that time. Like, it was a situation to help each other. I wasn't doing very well with my finances and living situation and he needed citizenship, he wasn't doing well with finding a better job, [um] he was educated but cleaning floors for like probably eight dollars ($8), you know . . . and he has children to take care of, and I know how that feels. So I was like, well, we can do this, I can help you with papers, you can help me with money. We agreed on it.*

Their analysis of potential risk and benefits involved in GCMF lacked strong factual foundations. All but one interviewed Americans believed GCMF would greatly influence (or would continue influencing) their financial situation. Fourteen of them expected to be a homeowner within a five-year period. Fifteen stated they hoped their lives would be stable and comfortable. Three hoped that money from GCMF would help them to start a business.[8] When taking into consideration the amount they received (or were still receiving) as a payment for their participation in fraud marriage, it was unlikely they would be able to achieve their dreams unless they found additional sources of income.

The research revealed that U.S. citizens not only overestimated the potential benefits but also underestimated the potential consequences of GCMF. They were less afraid of potential consequences for their participation in GCMF than immigrants were. Only five interviewed citizens feared consequences of GCMF. The remaining 12 stated that they were not afraid of being arrested and charged with GCMF or they did not think about it. U.S. citizens had a lower level of knowledge of the criminal consequences of marriage fraud. Eight out of 17 interviewed citizens admitted to having no knowledge of the consequences of GCMF. The remaining nine said they knew the criminal consequences of marriage fraud. But only three had factual knowledge about these consequences.

Marriage fraud brokers had similar reasons for engaging in GCMF as did U.S. citizens. All three brokers participated in GCMF for financial gain. They knew exactly how much money they could expect from each transaction and, unlike U.S. citizens, they always got their share. Additionally, Naomi and Steven stressed that "helping others" was also a very important motivation. So, for marriage brokers the benefits included a combination of financial gain as well as perceived altruism that made them feel good about themselves.

Despite marriage fraud brokers' clear understanding of benefits, their knowledge about the consequences of GCMF was not as clear. Penalties for engaging in GCMF for marriage fraud brokers are much more severe than for participating spouses (see Chapter 1). However, two interviewed brokers did not know about these higher penalties and did not want to hear about them. They were aware of their engagement in a serious criminal activity but were not interested in knowing about the courts sentencing options. Lack of knowledge helped them manage the fear of being caught. According to them, not knowing made their participation in GCMF easier. The third broker was somehow aware of consequences but expected the punishment to be less severe than it really is. When analyzing benefits and risks of engagement in GCMF, the lack of knowledge about the consequences helped the benefits outweigh the risks.

Although rational choice theory states that people weigh the risks and benefits of committing a crime, it does not assume that their evaluation of the risks is based on accurate information. Poor or inaccurate knowledge of the consequences of GCMF as well as overrated benefits do not eliminate a rational choice process. Significantly, the U.S. citizens understood that they engaged in a criminal behavior punishable by law and that for this behavior, they would be rewarded financially. They accepted risks of potential punishment in exchange for expected benefits, so they made a rational decision.

NOTES

1. In 1990, the U.S. government enacted a statute that conferred on Salvadoran asylum applicants a temporary protective status (TPS). Thanks to this status Salvadoran immigrants could reside and work in the United States on a limited basis (see Argueta and Wasem, 2016).

2. As discussed in Chapter 7 the immigrants understanding of *"the only way"*/*"the only option"* was ambiguous. Some understand it literally (this is truly the only path they know that gives them a chance to legalize their immigration status) and others figuratively (this is the best path to legal status they are aware of or the most reasonable under the current circumstance; it does not mean it is the only existing pathway). For six interviewed immigrants GCMF was literally the only option available, and four immigrants were aware of other options but perceived them achieved in their case.

3. To express opinions about the impact of U.S. legal system on their personal situation, interviewees used words such as: government, state, laws, and politicians.

4. Deficiencies regarding proper housing options were cited by the interviewees, including: complaints about limited housing availability for young mothers; long waiting time to be placed in the housing for low-income families; insufficient rental assistance programs; the poor locations of subsidized apartments (e.g., locations far from city centers, making it difficult to get a job without a car); and the conditions of homeless shelters.

5. Unless the person will be found guilty of a crime.

6. More details on this issue are presented in the Chapter 7, subsection "Knowledge about Legal Consequences of Green Card Marriage Fraud."

7. Mean income of this group is $1,056.7 per month.

8. Interviewees were asked how the GCMF would affect their lives within five years and where they saw themselves in five years.

Chapter Ten

Conclusions and Recommendations

This study has explored the experiences of people participating in Green Card Marriage Fraud (GCMF) and informed a theoretical model grounded in data that helped to explain why and how immigrants engage in marriage fraud. It developed new insight into this understudied phenomenon through the personal accounts of the study's informants, revealing a wide range of social and legal factors that are associated with the process of participating in GCMF. The information provided by the marriage fraud brokers was especially revelatory. As a consequence of America's political divide and on-going health crisis, the significance of GCMF phenomenon is likely to increase.

Although the narratives provided by the GCMF participants could not serve as a representative sample, their insider perspectives have permitted a first look at the population involved in GCMF, an important starting point for future research. Fifty-eight GCMF participants were targeted by the researcher (this number includes those who agreed to be interviewed and those who did not). The majority of targeted immigrants were African-American men, non-Hispanics, and were in their twenties, while the majority of U.S. citizens were African-American women, non-Hispanic and in their twenties. These characteristics are true for both populations in this study, targeted and interviewed population, as well as targeted but not interviewed. Additionally, most of the immigrants who agreed to participate in the interview were college graduates, full-time employees, and rarely had children. On the other hand, the majority of U.S. citizens participating in this study had some college experience, worked full-time but in low-wage jobs, already had children, and were experiencing financial hardship.

Generalization from the present study was not possible. Perhaps, researchers with greater means or those who may possess better access to this population will be able to recruit a representative sample of those involved in GCMF. Hopefully, this will occur and until such time it will be difficult to generalize about demographics of GCMF participants.

Nevertheless, the present research study found that none of the interviewed immigrants engaged in any illegal activity other than participation in GCMF. All of them entered the United States through ports of entry with valid visas. Five immigrants were holders of expired J1 visas (exchange visitors) when they engaged in GCMF, two had B2 visas (visitor), and two F1 (academic students) visas. Only one participant got married before the expiration of her visa. No differences were observed between those who engaged in the process of GCMF before and after visa expiration. Those who entered the United States with visas had to undergo a rigorous screening process. The U.S. Department of State collects and verifies information about applicants' demographics, previous travels, family background, ties to one's own country, education and training, work experience, criminal background and information relating to reasons, length of planned stay in the United States and financial capacity to cover travel expenses.[1] While Vazquez (2015) and Stumpf (2006) indicated that immigrants have been often equated with criminal offenders, the current research showed that immigrants are law-abiding individuals, and GCMF is the only criminal activity they have engaged in.

Most of the interviewed immigrants (eight) used cost-benefit analysis to justify migration. Their main push factors were the lack of employment and educational opportunities, and avenues to make money in their countries of origin. Immigrants from Haiti and Colombia considered their countries as dangerous, which motivated them to migrate. Additionally, one immigrant moved to the United States temporarily in order to attend college.

After or in anticipation of the expiration of their visas, the immigrants in the United States consciously decided to find a way to legalize their stay. For the majority of new immigrants, family or friends stepped into the role of advisers in regard to GCMF. Moreover, 13 U.S. citizens and eight immigrants were assisted by marriage fraud brokers.

All 10 immigrants perceived GCMF as the only option available for them to become a Legal Permanent Resident. Seven immigrants saw GCMF as the opportunity to improve their socioeconomic status and to further their educational opportunities, three as a chance to get health insurance, be able to support family in their countries of origin, and simply feel better without a constant fear of being apprehended and deported. U.S. citizens and marriage fraud brokers engaged in GCMF mainly for financial gain but also to help people better their lives.

The study also found that Cornish and Clarke's (1987) rational choice theory and Sykes and Matza's (1957) neutralization theory can be successfully used to help to understand peoples' decisions to participate in GCMF.

Knowing more about this population and why they engage in GCMF can help in development of policies that will prevent further expansion of this criminal activity. More research should be conducted in this area to explore fully the profiles of GCMF participants. This knowledge could help USCIS officers to distinguish more efficiently bona fide marriages from those undertaken for the sole purpose of obtaining a Green Card.

The severe civil and criminal consequences of marriage fraud should successfully deter potential offenders from engaging in this activity. However, the research uncovered that participants' knowledge of these consequences is generally minimal or inaccurate. Eight interviewed U.S. citizens and seven immigrants admitted having no knowledge of the consequences of GCMF. Nine U.S. citizens and three immigrants stated that they were aware of potential penalties for their involvement in GCMF. However, within this group, only three U.S. citizens and one immigrant expected a penalty similar to that provided by law. Since lack of proper knowledge about the consequences of GCMF may impact the deterrence effect of current policies, new preventive actions should be initiated with the purpose of educating people of the potential consequences of GCMF.

Moreover, this research revealed some consistent patterns in the marriage process between immigrants and U.S. citizens engaging in GCMF. Certain signs or indicators of these patterns could be observed during interviews with USCIS officers or could be targeted through analysis of documents submitted to prove the existence of a bona fide marriage. For example, none of the study's participants used religious services. All of them requested a ceremony performed by an in-state justice of the peace. They often requested a "Marriage without Delay" or scheduled a marriage ceremony in about a month.

All interviewees submitted to USCIS pictures of their wedding ceremony (as a proof of their bona fide marriage). Wedding pictures revealed some important details that may suggest increased likelihood of GCMF. For example, this research found that the majority of future spouses dressed casually during their wedding ceremony and had no wedding rings to exchange or had only very cheap rings. They brought only two to four friends with them but no family members (with the exception of siblings).[2] These details can be often seen in the pictures. Newlyweds usually go separate ways immediately after the ceremony and do not have wedding parties or honeymoons. Lack of pictures from these important moments should raise suspicions about the possibility of GCMF.

There was also a clear pattern in the type of documents GCMF spouses submitted to USCIS with the Form I-130. First, interviewed spouses were not able to provide any proof of joint ownership. They also had no children together, and therefore could not provide birth certificates. GCMF couples

usually showed that they lived in apartments that were previously rented by
an immigrant-spouse, and only after the marriage did the U.S. citizen-spouse
move in. Significantly, these couples were not likely to have any history of
living together prior to their marriage.[3] The only proof of combined financial
resources that they were generally able to produce was a joint bank account.
However, these bank accounts had little, if any activity. Spouses did not
deposit their salaries to these joint accounts or accumulate savings within
them. Moreover, account history can often reveal that money is deposited to
the account multiple times in a specific location, usually at an ATM or bank
close to the residency of the immigrant-spouse. Shortly thereafter, the money
is withdrawn at a different location which is likely to be the real residential
area of the U.S. citizen-spouse. In other words, account history has a potential
to reveal the pattern of payments for GCMF from immigrant to U.S. citizen.

Furthermore, knowing that couples prepare for the immigration interview
together, and base their preparation on questions available on the internet,
suggests that the interview process could benefit from a refreshed format and
content. New procedures could be developed to assure more accurate verification of bona fide marriages. During interviews, USCIS officers could ask
questions that were not previously published online. This would only create
additional obstacles for those persons involved in GCMF.

This study also explored whether GCMF can be classified as organized
crime. It was found that GCMF has a recognizable organizational structure,
although some marriage fraud brokers had more decision-making power than
others. Brokers also used paid recruiters who helped them target and convince
U.S. citizens to participate in GCMF. Marriage brokers collaborated with
each other, as well as with external players such as justices of the peace and
immigration attorneys. This in turn, exposed some involvement in corruption.
Such collaborations among brokers and other legitimate parties and the active
involvement of these parties in GCMF is one of the most surprising findings
of this study. This area deserves further in-depth exploration as it may play
a significant role in weakening the U.S. immigration system and sabotaging
the work of USCIS officers.

GCMF involves other elements of organized crime. U.S. citizens and
marriage fraud brokers engaged in this activity mainly for financial gain.
They operated like business enterprises. Their decisions were rational from
a business perspective, focused on increasing profits while decreasing risks
involved in their activities. Further research on the place of GCMF in the
organized crime structure is recommended.

Immigration seems to be a critical and prominent wedge issue in the
United States. The situation of current and future immigrants in the United
States is undergoing major changes. President Donald J. Trump has signed

several executive orders affecting immigration policy. The first order, *Border Security and Immigration Enforcement Improvements*,[4] focuses on border security. Section 4 of the executive order directs the Department of Homeland Security (DHS) to take immediate steps to allocate available funds, plan, design, and construct a physical wall on the U.S.-Mexico border. Section 8 directs DHS to hire an additional 5,000 Border Patrol agents. Sections 5 and 6 call for increased construction of detention facilities and detention of immigrants. Section 11 expands the application of "expedited removal" and limits access to asylum.

The second immigration-related executive order, *Enhancing Public Safety in the Interior of the United States*,[5] focuses on interior enforcement. Sections 5 and 7 of this order expand definitions of those unauthorized immigrants prioritized for removal and orders increases in enforcement personnel and removal facilities. Section 9 forbids "sanctuary" jurisdictions from receiving federal grants, except those that are necessary for enforcement purposes. Section 10 terminates the Priority Enforcement Program[6] and reinstitutes the Secure Communities program.[7]

The third executive order, *Protecting the Nation from Foreign Terrorist Entry into the United States*,[8] focuses on terrorism prevention. This executive order lowered the number of refugees to be admitted into the United States in 2017 to 50,000; bans nationals from Iran, Iraq, Libya, Somalia, Sudan, and Yemen from entering the United States for at least 90 days; blocks nationals from Syria indefinitely; and suspends the U.S. refugee program for 120 days.

While President Trump's executive orders have affected the situation of immigrants in the United States, on September 5, 2017, he also took steps to repeal of Deferred Action for Childhood Arrivals program (DACA). DACA is a kind of administrative relief from deportation. Its purpose is to protect eligible immigrant youth,[9] who came to the United States when they were children, from deportation and provide them with an opportunity to get a work permit. The rescission was challenged in court by different entities, but finally, on June 18, 2020, the Supreme Court ruled against the Trump administration's attempt to rescind DACA. The ruling emphasized that the administration failed to provide an adequate reason for its action as required by the *Administrative Procedure Act* (DHS et al. v. Regents of Univ. of Cal. et al., 2020). Following this decision, on July 17, 2020, the first court made this requirement to the DHS. District Court Judge Paul W. Grimm issued orders that required DHS to restore the DACA program to its pre-rescission status, prior to September 2017. However, on July 28, 2020, acting Secretary of Homeland Security Chad F. Wolf announced that they will not process new applications for the DACA program and that it will limit the renewal term for current DACA recipients to one year instead of the usual two (DHS,

2020). Moreover, President Trump is still working on the plans to limit family-based immigration, which he calls "chain migration" (realDonaldTrump, 2017). The impact of these policies to the crimmigration nexus should call for further research.

In the light of all these changes to the immigration system that occurred in 2017 and are still occurring in 2020, immigrants' fear of uncertainty is increasing. Naomi, a marriage fraud broker, was interviewed in summer of 2016, at the beginning of the presidential campaign. She was asked how many people she helped during 14 years of her GCMF business, and she said:

Thousands, thousands. I am doing at least two (2)—three (3) marriages a week. But now during presidential times [presidential campaigns] I get tremendously more. Elections, elections [ohh]! My phone is ringing horribly. All the time. Elections is a really big green light for me. That's when a lot of calls come.

She was asked to provide an explanation why she is getting more customers during elections. Naomi expounded:

Election because you don't know who gonna be president next. You don't know what the rules are gonna be. You don't know how they gonna change the system. That's the reason. They [immigrants] make it [decision to engage in GCMF] quicker when the scared. But first, just so you know, if Donald Trump is president my price goes up. And I mean it! I'm not voting on Donald but if he wins hell yea!- my price goes up. You've got a man who felt in love with immigrant and said he will build a wall. It's gonna be hard as fuck! Hard as shit to do my job. You know. So yea, I'm charging extra because it's gonna be a bigger risk for me to take. Shit! I've got a kid to live for [laughter]. But hey, the more they scared [immigrants] the more they pay.

Naomi's explanation proved that more restrictive policies, lack of opportunities to act within the law, and most of all, fear of an unstable immigration system that has a potential to become stricter, increases the number of people who decide to participate in GCMF.

As indicated in Chapter 2, economic and social insecurities that come from having an illegal immigration status increase stress, have a negative impact on one's psychological well-being, increase the risk of perpetrating intimate partner violence (Counts, Brown, and Campbell, 1999), and increase the likelihood of children being raised in poverty and unstable living arrangements (Landale, Thomas, and Van Hook, 2011). As immigrants (especially those without a legal status) observe changes in the current immigration system, they understand that their options for legal stay in the United States are shrinking.

When asked about the reasons behind the decision to get involved in GCMF, eight out of ten immigrants interviewed for this study said, *"that was the only way"* or *"the only option."* This shows that lack of options to act in accordance with the law push people to engage in illegal behaviors. Immigrants stripped of opportunities to remain legally in the United States, uncertain about their future, and scared of the unknown are more likely to look at GCMF as their only option. Moreover, marriage fraud brokers have an easier job to do recruiting potential participants to engage in GCMF among those who feel hopeless and are ready to catch any opportunity that can lead them to legal residency in the United States. The interviewed marriage fraud brokers are successfully developing their illegal businesses, improving their techniques to deceive immigration officials, and getting more clients. These findings should serve as a warning sign that GCMF has the potential to develop into a strong branch of organized crime.

NOTES

1. Based on Online Nonimmigrant Visa Application form (DS-160) filled by all immigrants who applied for nonimmigrant visas. All visas used by study participants (F1, J1, and B2 visas) are considered nonimmigrant.

2. It is important to note that these characteristics are not exclusively attributed to GCMF participants. Accumulation of these characteristics may provide a reason to take a closer look at a specific case of the marriage between immigrant and U.S. citizen, but should not lead to direct conclusions. More research should be done exploring all arrangements between spouses associated with GCMF.

3. USCIS can easily verify this pattern by requesting immigrants provide a tenancy agreement covering one year prior to marriage (joint or single). Both spouses are already required to provide their residence addresses for the last five years, as a part of G-325A, Biographic Information form that both spouses are required to complete. Based on the addresses of both spouses it can be determined if the U.S. citizen moved to the apartment rented by an immigrant-spouse and if the couple has any history of living together prior to marriage.

4. Executive Order 13767, titled *Border Security and Immigration Enforcement Improvements*, was signed by U.S. President Donald Trump on January 25, 2017. Text of this executive order is available under the following link https://www .whitehouse.gov/presidential-actions/executive-order-border-security-immigration -enforcement-improvements/.

5. Executive Order 13768, titled *Enhancing Public Safety in the Interior of the United States*, was signed by U.S. President Donald Trump on January 25, 2017. Text of this executive order is available under the following link https://www.whitehouse .gov/presidential-actions/executive-order-enhancing-public-safety-interior-united -states/.

6. Priority Enforcement Program was announced by DHS Secretary Jeh Johnson in a November 20, 2014 memo as a replacement for Secure Communities. The program worked with state and local law enforcement to identify aliens who come in contact with state or local law enforcement and remove those who are removable (either because their presence is unauthorized, or because they committed an aggravated felony).

7. Secure Communities is a deportation program that relies on partnership among federal, state, and local law enforcement agencies. ICE is the program manager. According to the ICE website "It uses a federal information-sharing partnership between DHS and the Federal Bureau of Investigation (FBI) that helps to identify in-custody aliens without imposing new or additional requirements on state and local law enforcement."

More about the program can be found under the link https://www.ice.gov/secure-communities.

8. Executive Order 13769, titled *Protecting the Nation from Foreign Terrorist Entry into the United States*, was signed by U.S. President Donald Trump. Except for the extent to which it was blocked by various courts, it was in effect from January 27, 2017, until March 16, 2017, when it was superseded by Executive Order 13780. Text of this executive order is available under the following link https://www.whitehouse.gov/presidential-actions/executive-order-protecting-nation-foreign-terrorist-entry-united-states/.

9. Eligible were those who: (1) Were under the age of 31 as of June 15, 2012; (2) Came to the United States before reaching their 16th birthday; (3) Have continuously resided in the United States since June 15, 2007, up to the present time; (4) Were physically present in the United States on June 15, 2012; (5) Had no lawful status on June 15, 2012; (6) Are currently in school, have graduated or obtained a certificate of completion from high school, have obtained a GED certificate, or are an honorably discharged veteran of the Coast Guard or Armed Forces of the United States; and (7) Have not been convicted of a felony, a significant misdemeanor, three or more other misdemeanors, and do not otherwise pose a threat to national security or public safety.

Recommendations

Even though this research did not use a representative sample, it is the first attempt to look at the population involved in Green Card marriage fraud (GCMF), thus an important starting point for future research. This study shows that those who engage in GCMF constitute a very unique group that deserves further attention from researchers. In-depth study of the literature revealed that GCMF is a greatly understudied crime. More research should be conducted to describe GCMF participants in more details using a representative sample which can be generalizable. Additionally, the role of marriage fraud brokers, justices of the peace, and other third parties in the GCMF process should be further explored.

This study focused on one type of GCMF called "cash-for-vows" where immigrants pay U.S. citizens for marriage in order to obtain resident status. However, there are more ways to arrange a fraudulent marriage. Such arrangements include: mail order bride arrangements, phony "arranged" marriages friends-and-family plans, "I do, I don't, I do" marriages, pop-up marriages for visa lottery winners, exploitative relationships, and heartbreakers. The Criminal Justice field would benefit from a deeper knowledge about all these types.

Research also exposed individuals' poor or inaccurate knowledge of the consequences of GCMF. Lack of proper knowledge may impact the deterrence effect of current policies. Therefore, new preventive actions should be initiated with the purpose of educating people about the consequences of GCMF.

Data acquired in this study may help to develop new procedures to assure more accurate verification of bona fide marriages. USCIS officers can take a more critical look at the documents provided during the "Adjustment of Status process." For example, they could seek for "alarming signs" on the photographs provided, require joint account history with all transactions listed and look for payments patterns, and conduct more home visits before the first immigration interview.[1] During the interview, USCIS officers could ask questions that were not previously published online.

The U.S. immigration system should develop a new pathway to Legal Permanent Residency with two main tracks. Those who already live on American soil (even without a legal permission to remain in the country) should be treated differently than newcomers. This research did not compare new or future immigrants with those who already have lived in the United States for a longer period of time, nor does it address differences between these groups. However, this research explored push and pull factors that led interviewed immigrants to migrate to the United States and to engage in GCMF. It is likely that stricter policies will deter from immigration to the United States those who are thinking about possible relocation, but still in their countries of origin. However, immigrants who are already successfully settled on American soil are likely to react differently to strict policies by turning to criminal activities such as GCMF. Immigrants appear to be more likely to participate in GCMF in times of uncertainty, especially when immigration policies are shifting against them.

The system would benefit from revised policies leading to "Legal Permanent Residency," provided strict requirements are met such as a clear background check, high school education (or GED), a level of competence in the English language, and the ability to fully financially support oneself. The Legal Permanent Residency could be granted temporarily to provide immigration officials an opportunity to evaluate immigrants' performance in the United States.

Moreover, a payment option for obtaining Legal Permanent Residency might be an additional requirement since some immigrants are already paying on average of eight thousand dollars ($8,000) to their spouses for fraud marriage. Additionally, they are paying other expenses associated with creating and maintaining a fraud marriage in order to deceive immigration officials. Immigrants were asked if they would legally purchase a Green Card if the U.S. government provided them with such an opportunity, and how much would they would be willing to pay for it; in this way, voiding the need to engage in a GCMF. Nine out of ten immigrants said they would be willing to pay for it. One immigrant said he could pay as much as $60,000 for it, five immigrants are willing to spend $50,000, two $20,000, and one no more than $10,000. Also, one interviewee stated that due to the fact that his GCMF process was so smooth and easy, he would still engage in it, even if there was a legal opportunity to purchase a Green Card.

At the same time, new procedures should be developed to prevent GCMF from reoccurring. Knowing how people deceive immigration officials should help to create new guidelines requiring different types of evidence to prove bona fide marriages. Multiple unexpected visits by immigration officials to the homes of spouses should be a new norm, helping to detect GCMF. Moreover, more research should be conducted to explore the role of justices of the peace, immigration lawyers, and other potential players who knowingly and intentionally aid and abet in GCMF.

GCMF and its social, legal, and political aspects are important factors in U.S. foreign and domestic affairs. These recommendations may help to inform future policy formation in the field of GCMF. Its participants form a hidden population which only seems to be enlarging.

NOTE

1. Home visits by U.S. immigration officers (called also "bed checks") can be conducted almost immediately after a filing of Adjustment of Status, after an interview has been completed, and even after the Green Card has already been approved. However, they are most likely to take place after the immigration interview. None of the study participants experienced a home visit before the interview.

A Statement of Limitation

All interviews—including interviews that were conducted for the present study—have some disadvantages that may cause a threat to research validity. Because it was understood that the researcher's presence may have biased responses, especially when the interview was recorded, this is a possible limitation of the research. All of the participants in this study have engaged in criminal activity (GCMF) in the past, or this activity was ongoing at the time when the interview was taking place; hence, their fear of disclosure could have caused them to hide some important information. To maximize her trustworthiness, the interviewer explained to participants how their confidentiality would be protected. The names of the participants and identifying information were not collected. Participants were given an alias name and were advised to use alias names to prevent identification of themselves or others. Whenever identifying information was inadvertently conveyed during the interview, it was deleted and not included in the transcription. Also, interviews took place at locations that would not arouse suspicion and that provided privacy for the conversation. Furthermore, participants did not have to answer all questions; they were advised that they could skip the question or even stop the interview whenever they felt uncomfortable. Before the interview began, the interviewer emphasized to participants that honest answers were really important; hence, they were told that it was better to skip the question than to provide a false answer.

Narrative responses were desired and therefore questions were open-ended. However, not all people are equally articulate and perceptive (Creswell, 2009). As expected, based on existing marriage fraud cases, most of the interviewed U.S. citizens participating in GCMF came from disadvantaged neighborhoods and had obtained only minimum levels of education. The use of slang during interviews was common. The interviews were recorded and then transcribed to help ensure that everything participants said was saved and correctly coded.

All interviews were conducted solely in English even though for immigrant participants English is usually a second language. However, fluency in English was anticipated because this is one of the requirements to obtain a Green Card. Participant consent forms were read aloud and explained to each participant. Though, no translation was provided. If a participant was not fluent in English, the interview was not conducted. Multiple strategies to assure mutual understanding were developed. The researcher prepared supporting questions to make sure that participants understood the question the way it was meant to be understood. Also, the researcher sought clarification if the answer provided was confusing or ambiguous.

There are also several challenges inherent in snowball sampling. Within the most important are limitations to generalizability. Since snowball sampling does not yield a random sample, the results from a study using this method are not generalizable to the population under study (Griffiths et al., 1993). Some researchers believe that it is impossible to make unbiased estimates from snowball samples (Heckathorn, 1997). But according to Cohen and Arieli (2011), a researcher can overcome limitations of snowball sampling and increase "the representativity of a snowball sample by sufficient planning of the sampling process and goals, initiating parallel snowball networks and using quota sampling" (p. 428).

In this study, most of the contacts with study participants were established with the help of marriage brokers. Thirteen out of 17 citizens and eight out of ten immigrants were assisted by marriage fraud brokers. Nineteen of them were navigated through the GCMF process by one of three Brokers participating in this study. Since the majority of study participants were coached by one of three marriage brokers, their patterns of offending and experiences may not be representative of the general population of those engaged in GCMF.

Moreover, it must be acknowledged that all three marriage fraud brokers were African Americans. Their clients were also mainly African Americans. It became apparent that brokers specialize in serving people of a particular background, usually similar to their own. Elizabeth said she accepts all kinds of customers but most of her clients were "*Black and Brown.*" Naomi focused on recruiting mostly West Africans, especially Nigerians. Also, Steven focused on Nigerians, but he specifically targeted students. This selective targeting was also responsible for low racial diversity in the study sample. Among all targeted GCMF participants, 21 were Caucasians, 32 African Americans, and five individuals who classified themselves as two or more races.

This study was built on experiences using a pre-test to identify any problems with interview questions and/or the data collection process prior to fielding the larger study. This pre-test involved collecting data from a relatively small number of participants (total of four people) and permanent evaluation of procedures and close monitoring of any human subject's issues that arose. There was ongoing evaluation of the demographic characteristics of the participants. Therefore, when the sample was too homogenous, additional procedures to increase representatively were applied. Problems with the homogeneity of the sample may be increased by parallel snowball networks and some use of quota sampling (Cohen and Arieli, 2011), as well as efforts to recruit a larger sample (Atkinson and Flint, 2001). In this study, the first method was applied.

The recruitment process started from three cultural guides (informants) known to the researcher. They were from different countries and cultural groups because it was expected that due to the nature of GCMF, this crime required some cooperation from family, friends, or other acquaintances. Therefore, immigrants who want to engage in GCMF are likely to look for information and assistance within their communities. Different communities develop unique patterns of dealing with GCMF. As expected, cultural guides are recommended for interview participants of the same nationality as their own. To gain access to a more diverse population and target various patterns of offending, the researcher had to restart the snowball sampling procedure twice by asking a GCMF broker for help to find participants from a different cultural group. There are also other methods known to greatly improve representativeness of the study sample such as sample weighting (Snijders, 1992) or more advanced "Respondent Driven Sampling" (Heckathorn, 1997). These methods were not applied in this study but are recommended for use in future research.

Despite the limitations inherent in snowball sampling, it has been suggested that it is the most effective method to access hidden or hard to reach populations (Valdez and Kaplan, 1999). When a population is unknown and there is little information available about it, this method can provide a better understanding and more complete characterization of a population. GCMF participants can be classified as a hidden population. There is very little known about this group and there is no existing sampling frame for them. The author was unable to identify a more representative sampling method for gaining access to this type of hidden population. Despite its challenges, snowball sampling was selected as an appropriate method to use for this study.

In the era when immigration has become such a polarizing topic, it is necessary to have access to credible data that will allow a better understanding and more complete characterization of a population. Immigration and Customs

Enforcement (ICE), an agency within the Department of Homeland Security, has identified immigration fraud as a growing problem: "Marriage fraud is a threat to U.S. national security, financial institutions and the integrity of the immigration system" (ICE, 2014b, p. 2). Hopefully, this study has expanded the body of scientific data available about GCMF and will help to encourage further research efforts. Up to date, there has been no qualitative research conducted focused on GCMF. The available research uses only official data based on revealed fraud marriages (when the Green Card is denied or when a person is prosecuted for a sham marriage before or after receiving a Green Card). Therefore, this study offers useful information and recommendations to be considered by researchers, to help further explore this hidden population. Moreover, the understanding of a growing scale of GCMF and its legal and political implications can influence policy change.

Bibliography

Abraham, M. (2000). *Speaking the Unspeakable*: *Marital Violence Among South Asian Immigrants in the United States*. New Brunswick, NJ: Rutgers University Press.

Abrams, K. (2012). Marriage Fraud. *California Law Review*, Vol. 100(1), 1–67.

Abrams, K. (2013). Citizen Spouse. *California Law Review*, Vol. 101(2), 407–444.

Agamben, G. (1995). *Homo Sacer: Sovereign Power and Bare Life* (Daniel Heller-Roazen, Trans.). Stanford, CA: Stanford University Press.

Agamben G. (2005). *State of Exception*, (Kevin Attell, Trans.). Chicago: The University of Chicago Press.

Andrews, T. (2012). What Is Social Constructionism? *The Grounded Theory Review*, Vol. 11(1), 39–46.

Argueta, C. N. and Wasem, R. E. (2016). Temporary Protected Status: Current Immigration Policy and Issues. Congressional Research Service, No 7-5700. Retrieved from https://www.fas.org/sgp/crs/homesec/RS20844.pdf.

Arnold, K. (2007). Enemy Invaders! Mexican Immigrants and U.S. Wars Against Them. Borderlands, Vol. 6(3). Retrieved from http://go.galegroup.com.libproxy .uml.edu/ps/i.do?id=GALE%7CA177943240&v=2.1&u=mlin_n_umass&it=r&p= STOM&sw=w&asid=4eb4c1ff499e2e8561a3297b5988e883.

Atkinson, R. and Flint, J. (2001). Accessing Hidden and Hard-to-Reach Populations: Snowball Research Strategies. *Social Research Update*, Vol. 33.

Baker, B. (2018). Population Estimates. Illegal Alien Population Residing in the United States: January 2015. Department of Homeland Security, Office of Immigration Statistics.

Bartram, D., Poros, M. V., and Monforte, P. (2014). *Key Concepts in Migration*. Los Angeles, CA: SAGE.

Batalova, J., McHugh, M., and Morawski, M. (2014). *Brain Waste in the US Workforce–Migration Policy Institute*: *Select Labor Force Characteristics of College-Educated Native-Born and Foreign-Born Adults*. Washington, DC: Migration Policy Institute.

Baum, S., and Flores, S. M. (2011). Higher Education and Children in Immigrant Families. *Future of Children*, Vol. 21(1), 171–193.

Benson, M. L. (1985). Denying the Guilty Mind: Accounting for Involvement in White-Collar Crime. *Criminology,* Vol. 23, 583–608.

Bentham, J. (1823). *An Introduction to the Principles of Morals and Legislation.* London: W. Pickering, 1823.

Biernacki, P. and Wardorf, D. (1981). Snowball Sampling, Problems and Techniques of Chain Referral Sampling. *Sociological Methods & Research,* Vol. 10(2), 141–163.

Black, R., Natali C., and Skinner, J. (2006). Migration and Inequality [Background Paper]. In: World Bank (ed.) *World Development Report 2006.* Washington, DC: World Bank.

Bloemraad, I. (2006). *Becoming a Citizen: Incorporating Immigrants and Refugees in the United States and Canada.* University of California Press, Berkeley.

Bornstein, M. and Bohr, Y. (2011). Immigration, Acculturation and Parenting. In *Encyclopedia on Early Childhood Development. Centre of Excellence for Early Childhood Development.*

Bucerius, S. M. and Tonry, M. H. (2014). *The Oxford Handbook of Ethnicity, Crime, and Immigration.* Oxford: Oxford University Press.

Bureau of Labor Statistics. (2015). Foreign-Born Workers: Labor Force Characteristics—2014. News Release. Retrieved from http://www.bls.gov/news.release/pdf/forbrn.pdf

Burridge, A. (2009). Differential Criminalization under Operation Streamline: Challenges to Freedom of Movement and Humanitarian Aid Provision in the Mexico-US Borderlands. *Refuge,* Vol. 26(2), 78–91.

Byers, B. D. and Crider, B. W. (2002). Hate Crimes Against the Amish: A Qualitative Analysis of Bias Motivation Using Routine Activities Theory. *Deviant Behavior,* Vol. 23, 115–148.

Camille, R. L. and Bauman, K. (2015). Educational Attainment in the United States: 2015 [report]. *United States Census Bureau.* Retrieved from https://www.census.gov/content/dam/Census/library/publications/2016/demo/p20-578.pdf.

Carlen, P. (1990). Alternatives to Women's Imprisonment. Milton Keynes [England]: Open University Press.

Charmaz, K. (2002). Qualitative Interviewing and Grounded Theory Analysis. In J. F. Gubrium and J. A. Holstein (eds.). *Handbook of Interview Research: Context and Method,* 675–693. Thousand Oaks: Sage.

Chi, M. and Drewianka, S. (2014). How Much Is a Green Card Worth? Evidence from Mexican Men Who Marry Women Born in the U.S. *Labour Economics*, Vol. 31, 103–116.

Cohen, N. and Arieli, T. (2011). Field Research in Conflict Environments: Methodological Challenges and Snowball Sampling. *Journal of Peace Research*, Vol. 48(4), 423–435.

Copes, H. (2003). Societal Attachments, Offending Frequency, and Techniques of Neutralization. *Deviant Behavior,* Vol. 24, 101–127.

Corbin, J., & Strauss, A. (2008). Basics of qualitative research: Techniques and procedures for developing grounded theory. Los Angeles: Sage.

Cornish, D. and Clarke, R. (1986). *The Reasoning Criminal.* New York: Springer-Verlag.

Cornish, D. and Clarke, R. (1987). Understanding Crime Displacement: An Application of Rational Choice Theory. *Criminology*, Vol. 25(4), 933–947.

Counts, D., Brown, J., and Campbell, J. (1999). *To Have and To Hit: Cultural Perspectives on Wife Beating.* Urbana, IL: University of Illinois Press.

Creswell, J. W. (1998). *Qualitative Inquiry and Research Design: Choosing Among Five Traditions.* Thousand Oaks, CA: Sage Publications.

Creswell, J. W. (2009). *Research Design: Qualitative, Quantitative, and Mixed Methods Approaches.* Los Angeles: Sage Publications.

Creswell, J. W., Hanson, W. E., Plan-Clark, V. L., and Morales, A. (2007). Qualitative Research Designs: Selection and Implementation. *The Counseling Psychologist,* Vol. 35, 236–264.

Cromwell, P. and Thurman, Q. (2003). The Devil Made Me Do It: Schematic Bases of Belief Change. In J.R. Eiser (ed.). *Attitudinal Judgement.* New York: Springer.

De Jong, G. F. and Fawcett, J. T. (1981). Motivations for Migration: An Assessment and a value expectancy research model. In G.F. De Jong and R.W. Gardner (eds.), *Migration Decision Making: Multidisciplinary Approaches to Microlevel Studies in Developed and Developing Countries* (pp. 13–58). New York: Pergamon.

Department of Homeland Security. (2014). I-9 Central. Completing Section 2, Employer Review and Verification.

Department of Homeland Security. (2018). *Yearbook of Immigration Statistics: 2018.* Washington, DC: U.S. Department of Homeland Security, Office of Immigration Statistics.

Department of Homeland Security. (2020). Department of Homeland Security Will Reject Initial Requests for DACA as It Weighs Future of the Program. Press Release. Retrieved from https://www.dhs.gov/news/2020/07/28/department-homeland-security-will-reject-initial-requests-daca-it-weighs-future#.

Department of Homeland Security et al. v. Regents of University of California et al., 18–587 (06/18/2020).

Drachman, D. and Paulino, A. (2004). *Immigrants and Social Work: Thinking Beyond the Borders of the United States.* Binghamton, NY: Routledge.

Edmonston, B., National Research Council (U.S.). (1996). *Statistics on U.S. immigration: An assessment of data needs for future research.* Washington, D.C: National Academy Press.

Entorf, H. (2000). Rational Migration Policy Should Tolerate Non-Zero Illegal Migration Flows: Lessons from Modelling the Market for Illegal Migration. Würzburg Economic Papers, No. 23. Retrieved from https://www.econstor.eu/dspace/bitstream/10419/48473/1/570611636.pdf.

Fan, M. (2013). The Case for Crimmigration Reform. *North Carolina Law Review,* Vol. 92(1), 75–148.

Fassinger, R. E. (2005). Paradigms, Praxis, Problems, and Promise: Grounded Theory in Counseling Psychology Research. *Journal of Counseling Psychology*, Vol. 52, 156–166.

FBI (n.d.) *Organized Crime Glossary*. Retrieved from https://www.fbi.gov/ investigate/organized-crime.

Ferraro, K. J. and Johnson, J. M. (1983). How Women Experience Battering: The Process of Victimization. *Social Problems*, Vol. 30(3), 325–339.

Freud, S. (1915). The Unconscious. *Standard Edition*, Vol. 41, 159–215.

Gallup. (July 16, 2014). One in Six Say Immigration Most Important U.S. Problem. [Graphs]. Retrieved from http://www.gallup.com/poll/173306/one-six-say -immigration-important-problem.aspx.

Garcia, A. S. and Keyes, D. (2012). *Life as an Undocumented Immigrant: How Restrictive Local Immigration Policies Affect Daily Life*. Washington DC: Center for American Progress.

García Hernández, C. C. (2013). Creating Crimmigration. *Brigham Young University Law Review*, Vol. 6, 1457–1515.

García Hernández, C. C. (2015). *Crimmigration Law*. ABA Book Publishing.

Glaser, B. G. and Strauss, A. L. (1967). *The Discovery of Grounded Theory; Strategies for Qualitative Research*. Chicago: Aldine.

Gleeson, S. and Gonzales, R. G. (2012). When Do Papers Matter? An Institutional Analysis of Undocumented Life in the United States. *International Migration*, Vol. 50(4), 1–19.

Golash-Boza, T. M. (2015). *Deported. Immigrant Policing, Disposable Labor, and Global Capitalism*. New York: New York University Press.

Griffiths, P., Gossop, M., Powis, B., and Strang, J. (1993). Researching Hidden Populations of Drug Users by Privileged Access Interviewers: Methodological and Practical Issues. *Addiction*, Vol. 88, 1617–1626.

Haberfeld, M. and Lieberman, C. A. (2012). Foreign Threats to National Security and an Alternative Model to Local Enforcement of US Immigration Laws. *Police Practice & Research: An International Journal*, Vol.13 (2), 155–166.

Hagan, F. E. (2006). "Organized Crime" and "Organized Crime": Indeterminate Problems of Definition. *Trends in Organized Crime*, Vol. 9(4), 127–137.

Hammar, T. (1990). *Democracy and the Nation State: Aliens, Denizens, and Citizens in a World of International Migration*. Aldershot, Hants, England: Avebury.

Hanson, G. H. (2012). Immigration and Economic Growth. *CATO Journal*, Vol. 32(1), 25–34.

Harris, J. R. and Todaro, M.P. (1970). Migration, Unemployment and Development: A Two-Sector Analysis. *American Economic Review*, Vol. 60(1), 126–142.

Haug, S. (2008). Migration Networks and Migration Decision-Making. *Journal of Ethnic and Migration Studies*, Vol. 34(4), 585–605.

Heckathorn, D. D. (1997). Respondent-Driven Sampling: A New Approach to the Study of Hidden Populations. *Social Problems*, Vol. 44, 174–199.

Higginson, J. G. (1999). Defining, Excusing, and Justifying Deviance: Teen Mothers' Accounts of Statutory Rape. *Symbolic Interaction*, Vol. 22, 25–44.

Hollinger, R. (1991). Neutralizing in the workplace: An Empirical Analysis of Property Theft and Production Deviance. *Deviant Behavior: An Interdisciplinary Journal*, Vol. 12(2), 169–202.

Holt, T. J. and Copes, H. (2010). Transferring Subcultural Knowledge On-Line: Practices and Beliefs of Persistent Digital Pirates. *Deviant Behavior*, Vol. 31(7), 625–654.

H.R. Rep. No. 99–906, at 6 (1986), reprinted in 1986 U.S.C.C.A.N. 5978, 5978.

ICE. U.S. Immigration and Customs Enforcement. (2014a). TOP STORY: ICE leading nationwide campaign to stop marriage fraud. Retrieved from https://www.ice.gov/news/releases/top-story-ice-leading-nationwide-campaign-stop-marriage-fraud.

ICE. U.S. Immigration and Customs Enforcement. (2014b). Marriage Fraud Brochure [PDF document]. Retrieved from http://www.ice.gov/sites/default/files/documents/Document/2014/marriageFraudBrochure.pdf.

Ikäheimo, O., Laukkanen, M., Hakko, H., and Räsänen, P. (2013). Association of Family Structure to Later Criminality: A Population-Based Follow-up Study of Adolescent Psychiatric Inpatients in Northern Finland. *Child Psychiatry & Human Development*, Vol. 44(2), 233–246.

Interview with USCIS officer, U.S. Citizenship & Immigration Serv., in Pittsburgh, PA (Sept. 26, 2012). In: A. Lernatovych. (2014). Breaking the Law to be Within the Law. *Duquesne Law Review*, Vol. 52, 209–229.

Ji, Q. and Batalova, J. (2012). College-Educated Immigrants in the United States. Migration Policy Institute. Retrieved from http://www.migrationpolicy.org/article/college-educated-immigrants-united-states.

Johnson, W. R., Morrow, P. C., and Johnson, G. J. (2002). An Evaluation of a Perceived Overqualification Scale across Work Settings. *The Journal of Psychology*, Vol. 136, 425–441. In Y. H. Roh, J. Y. Chang, M. U. Kim, and S. K. Nam. (2014). The Effects of Income and Skill Utilization on the Underemployed's Self-Esteem, Mental Health, and Life Satisfaction. *Journal Of Employment Counseling*, Vol. 51(3), 125–141.

Kahn, L. J. and Morrow, P. C. (1991). Objective and Subjective Underemployment Relationships to Job Satisfaction. *Journal of Business Research*, Vol. 22, 211–218. In Y. H. Roh, J. Y. Chang, M. U. Kim, and S. K. Nam. (2014). The Effects of Income and Skill Utilization on the Underemployed's Self-Esteem, Mental Health, and Life Satisfaction. *Journal of Employment Counseling*, Vol. 51(3), 125–141.

Killawi, Y. (2013). Preserving an Entrepreneurial America: How Restrictive Immigration Policies Stifle the Creation and Growth of Startups and Small Businesses. *Entrepreneurial Business Law Journal*, Vol. 8(1), 129–157.

Koff, H. (2008). *Fortress Europe or a Europe of Fortresses? The Integration of Migrants in Western Europe*. Bruxelles: P.I.E. Peter Lang.

Landale, N., Thomas, K. J., and Van Hook, J. (2011). The Living Arrangements of Children of Immigrants. *Future Child*. Vol. 21(1), 43–70.

Lernatovych, A. (2014). Breaking the Law to be Within the Law. *Duquesne Law Review*, Vol. 52, 209–229.

Lewis v. United States. (2006). 518 U.S. 322, 326.

López-Sander, L. (2014). Economic Benefits and Costs of Immigration. In J. Ciment & J. Radzilowski (Eds). *American Immigration: An Encyclopedia of Political, Social, and Cultural Change* (271–274), Armonk, NY: M.E. Sharpe.

Lowdermilk, E. and Brunache, J. (2013). Experiencing Unexpected Pathways: A Grounded Theory Study of the Surprising Transformation of Inner-City Youth. *Social Work & Christianity*, Vol. 40(3), 322–351.

Lutwak et al. v. United States, 344 U.S. 604 (1953).

Lydgate, J. (2010). Assembly-Line Justice: A Review of Operation Streamline. *California Law Review*, Vol. 98(2), 481–544.

Marcum, C. D., Higgins, G. E., Wolfe, S. E., and Ricketts, M. L. (2011). Examining the Intersection of Self-Control, Peer Association and Neutralization in Explaining Digital Piracy. *Western Criminology Review*, Vol. 12(3), 60–74.

Massey, D. S. (2010). Immigration Statistics for the 21st Century. The Annals of the American Academy of *Political and Social Science*, Vol. 631(1), 124–140.

Maynard, D. C., Joseph, T. A., and Maynard, M. (2006). Underemployment, Job Attitudes, and Turnover Intentions. *Journal of Organizational Behavior*, Vol. 27, 509–536. In Y. H. Roh, J. Y. Chang, M. U. Kim, and S. K. Nam. (2014). The Effects of Income and Skill Utilization on the Underemployed's Self-Esteem, Mental Health, and Life Satisfaction. *Journal of Employment Counseling*, Vol. 51(3), 125–141.

McCrory M. L. (2006, December 23). Organizer of Sham Marriages Sentenced. The Washington Post, Retrieved from www.lexisnexis.com/hottopics/lnacademic.

Messerschmidt, J. W. (1993). Masculinities and Crime: Critique and Reconceptualization of Theory. Lanham, MD: Rowman and Littlefield Publishers.

Migration Policy Institute Data Hub. (2011). *An Earnings and Poverty Profile of US Immigrants.* Retrieved from https://www.migrationpolicy.org/data/state-profiles/state/income/US.

Miller, T. (2003). Citizenship and Severity: Recent Immigration Reforms and the New Penology. *Georgetown Immigration Law Journal*, Vol. 17, 611– 666.

Moore, R. and McMullan, E. C. (2009). Neutralizations and Rationalizations of Digital Piracy: A Qualitative Analysis of University Students. *International Journal of Cyber Criminology*, Vol. 3(1), 441–451.

Morris, R. G., & Higgins, G. E. (2009). Neutralizing Potential and Self-Reported Digital Piracy: A Multitheoretical Exploration Among College Undergraduates. *Criminal Justice Review*, Vol. 34(2), 173–195.

Morse, J. M. (1994). Designing funded qualitative research. In N. K. Denizin and Y. S. Lincoln. *Handbook of Qualitative Research (2nd Ed).* Thousand Oaks, CA: Sage.

National Research Council. (2005). Policy Implications of International Graduate Students and Postdoctoral Scholars in the United States. Washington DC: National Academy Press.

Naiditch, C., Tomini, A. and Ben Lakhdar, C. (2015). Remittances and Incentive to Migrate: An Epidemic Approach of Migration. *International Economics*, Vol. 142, 118–135.

North, D. (2013). More on Fighting Immigration-Related Marriage Fraud. Center for Immigration Studies. Backgrounders and Reports. Retrieved from http://cis.org/north/more-fighting-immigration-related-marriage-fraud.

Ortega, D. M. and Lasch, C. N. (2014). Crimmigration and Detainers: An Opportunity for Feminist Praxis. *Affilia: Journal of Women & Social Work.* Vol. 23(3), 257–260.

Padgett Torres, S. (2014). U.S. Citizenship and Immigration Services: Investigating and Preventing Immigration Marriage Fraud. Forensics Journal. Stevenson University, 20–25. Retrieved from http://www.joomag.com/magazine/forensics-journal -stevenson-university-2014/0902791001400507253?page=21.

Peretti-Watel, P. (2003). Neutralization theory and the denial of risk: some evidence from cannabis use among French adolescents. *The British Journal of Sociology*, Vol.54(1), 21-42.

Pogrebin, M., Stretesky, P. B., Unnithan, N. P., and Venor, G. (2006). Retrospective Accounts of Violent Events by Gun Offenders. *Deviant Behavior*, Vol. 27, 479–501.

Pope, P. J. and Garrett, T. M. (2012). America's Homo Sacer: Examining U.S. Deportation Hearings and the Criminalization of Illegal Immigration. *Administration & Society*, Vol. 45(2), 167–186.

Porter, L. (2006). Illegal Immigrants Should Not Receive Social Services. *International Social Science Review*, Vol. 81(1/2), 66–72.

Portes, A. and Rumbaut, R. G. (2006). *Immigrant America: A Portrait.* University of California Press, Berkeley.

Presser, L. (2004). Violent Offenders, Moral Selves: Constructing Identities and Accounts in the Research Interview. *Social Problems*, Vol. 51, 82–102.

Priest, T. B. and McGrath, J. H. (1970). Techniques of Neutralization: Young Adult Marijuana Smokers. *Criminology,* Vol. 8(2), 185–194.

realDonaldTrump (2017, September 15). CHAIN MIGRATION Cannot be Allowed to be Part of Any Legislation on Immigration! [Tweet]. Retrieved from https://twitter.com/realDonaldTrump/status/908676979561570304.

Reitz, J. G. (1998). *Warmth of the Welcome: The Social Causes of Economic Success for Immigrants in Different Nations and Cities.* Boulder, CO: Westview Press.

Rumbaut, R. G. and Ewing, W. A. (2007). The Myth of Immigrant Criminality and the Paradox of Assimilation: Incarceration Rates Among Native and Foreign-Born Men (Immigration Policy Center Special Report) Washington, DC: American Immigration Law Foundation.

Ryo, E. (2015). Less Enforcement, More Compliance: Rethinking Unauthorized Migration. *UCLA Law Review,* Vol. 62(3), 622–670.

Salehyan, I. (2008). The Externalities of Civil Strife: Refugees as a Source of International Conflict. *American Journal of Political Science*, Vol. 52(4), 787–801.

Scully, D. and Marolla, J. (1984). Convicted Rapists' Vocabulary of Motive: Excuses and Justifications. *Social Problems*, Vol. 31(5), 530–544.

Sefiha, O. (2012). Bike Racing, Neutralization, and the Social Construction of Performance-Enhancing Drug Use. *Contemporary Drug Problems,* Vol. 39(2), 213–245.

Segal, U. A. and Mayadas, N. S. (2005). *Assessment of Issues Facing Immigrant and Refugee Families.* Child Welfare League of America.

Seminara, D. (2008). Hello, I Love You, Won't You Tell Me Your Name: Inside the Green Card Marriage Phenomenon. Center for Immigration Studies. Backgrounders and Reports (November 2008). Retrieved from http://cis.org/marriagefraud.

Shaw, J. (2007). The Transformation of Citizenship in the European Union: Electoral Rights and the Restructuring of Political Space. Cambridge, MA: Cambridge University Press.

Simon, S. (Host). (April 18, 2020). Immigrant Doctors Face Barriers Trying to Volunteer to Help Fight COVID-19 Pandemic. *NPR. Weekend Edition Saturday* [Radio broadcast episode]. Retrieved from https://www.npr.org/2020/04/18/837855173/immigrant-doctors-face-barriers-trying-to-volunteer-to-help-fight-covid-19-pandemic.

Sjaastad, L. A. (1962). The costs and Returns of Human Migration. *The Journal of Political Economy*, Vol. 70(5), 80–93.

Sklansky, D. A. (2012). Crime, Immigration, and Ad Hoc Instrumentalism. *New Criminal Law Review: An International and Interdisciplinary Journal*, Vol. 15, 157–223.

Snijders, T. A. B. (1992). Estimation in the Basis of Snowball Samples: How to Weight? *Bulletin of Sociological Methodology*, Vol.36(1), 59–70.

Strauss, A. L. and Corbin, J. M. (1998). *Basics of Qualitative Research: Grounded Theory Procedures and Techniques* (2nd ed.). Newbury Park, CA: SAGE.

Stumpf, J. (2006). The Crimmigration Crisis: Immigrants, Crime, and Sovereign Power. *American University Law Review*, Vol. 56(2), 367–419.

Sullivan, D. H. and Ziegert, A. L. (2008). Hispanic Immigrant Poverty: Does Ethnic Origin Matter? *Population Research and Policy Review*, Vol. 27(6), 667–687.

Sykes, G. and Matza, D. (1957). Techniques of Neutralization: A Theory of Delinquency. *American Sociological Review*, Vol. 22(6), 664–670.

Talwar, G., Sianko, N., Baugh, S.-A. and Brodsky, A. E. (2012). Talking about immigration: Community voices on service, research, and policy needs. *American Journal of Orthopsychiatry*, Vol. 82(3), 431–436.

The White House, Office of the Press Secretary. (November 20, 2014). FACT SHEET: Immigration Accountability Executive Action. Retrieved from https://obamawhitehouse.archives.gov/the-press-office/2014/11/20/fact-sheet-immigration-accountability-executive-action.

Time. (March 29–30, 2006). Retrieved from http://www.pollingreport.com/immigration.htm. In G. Lahav and M. Courtemanche (2012). The Ideological Effects of Framing Threat on Immigration and Civil Liberties. *Political Behavior,* Vol. 34(3), 477–505.

Todaro, M. P. (1976). *Internal Migration in Developing Countries: A Survey.* Geneva: International Labor Office.

TRAC Immigration. (April 8, 2014). Secure Communities and ICE Deportations: A Failed Program?. Retrieved from http://trac.syr.edu/immigration/reports/349/.

Treverton, G. F., Matthies, C., Cunningham, K. J., Goulka, J., Ridgeway, G., and Wong, A. (2009). *Film Piracy, Organized Crime, and Terrorism*. Santa Monica, CA: RAND.

Trujillo-Pagán, N. (2014). Emphasizing the 'Complex' in the 'Immigration industrial complex.' *Critical Sociology*, Vol. 40, 29–46.

United States. (1980). Immigration and Nationality Act, with Amendments and Notes on Related Laws: Committee Print for the Use of the Committee on the Judiciary, House of Representatives, United States. Washington: U.S. G.P.O.

United States Census Bureau (2015). PINC-01. Selected Characteristics of People 15 Years and Over, by Total Money Income, Work Experience, Race, Hispanic

Origin, and Sex. [data]. Retrieved from https://www.census.gov/data/tables/time -series/demo/income-poverty/cps-pinc/pinc-01.2015.html.

United States Census Bureau (2018a). Place of Birth by Nativity and Citizenship Status TableID: B05002 [data]. Retrieved from https://data.census.gov/cedsci/ table?q=B05002&tid=ACSDT1Y2018.B05002.

United States Census Bureau (2018b). Poverty Status of Families by Family Type, Nativity, and U.S. Citizenship Status of the Householder. Table 1.14. [data]. Retrieved from https://www.census.gov/data/tables/2019/demo/foreign-born/cps -2019.html.

United States Citizenship and Immigration Service. (2015). Exchange Visitors. Retrieved from https://www.uscis.gov/working-united-states/students-and-exchange -visitors/exchange-visitors.

United States Citizenship and Immigration Service. (2016). Students and Employment. Retrieved from https://www.uscis.gov/working-united-states/students-and -exchange-visitors/students-and-employment.

United States Citizenship and Immigration Service. (2018). Number of I-130 Alien Relative Petitions by Category of Relatives, Case Status, and USCIS Field Office or Service Center Location. 1st Qtr, 2nd Qtr, 3rd Qtr, and 4th Qtr. [Data file]. Retrieved from https://www.uscis.gov/sites/default/files/document/data/I130_ performancedata_fy2018_qtr1.pdf.

United States Citizenship and Immigration Service. (2019a). Instructions for Form I-130, Petition for Alien Relative, and Form I-130A, Supplemental Information for Spouse Beneficiary. OMB No. 1615-0012. Retrieved from https://www.uscis.gov/ sites/default/files/document/forms/i-130instr.pdf.

United States Citizenship and Immigration Services. (2019b). Our History. Retrieved from https://www.uscis.gov/history-and-genealogy/our-history.

United States Citizenship and Immigration Service. (2020a). Green Card. Retrieved from http://www.uscis.gov/greencard.

United States Citizenship and Immigration Service. (2020b). While Your Green Card Application Is Pending with USCIS. Retrieved from https://www.uscis.gov/green -card/while-your-green-card-application-is-pending-with-uscis.

United States Department of Education, Federal Student Aid, Customer Experience Group. (2012). Funding Your Education The Guide to Federal Student Aid. Retrieved from https://studentaid.ed.gov/sa/sites/default/files/2012-13-funding-your -education.pdf.

U.S. Department of State. (2016). Visitor Visa. Retrieved from https://travel.state. gov/content/visas/en/visit/visitor.html.

U.S. Senate S.1720. 115th Congress (2017–2018). RAISE Act. Summary. Retrieved from https://www.congress.gov/bill/115th-congress/senate-bill/1720?q=%7B%22 search%22%3A%5B%22raise+act%22%5D%7D&r=1.

Valdez, A. and Kaplan, C. D. (1999). Reducing Selection Bias in the Use of Focus Groups to Investigate Hidden Populations: The Case of Mexican-American Gang Members from South Texas. *Drugs and Society,* Vol. 14, 209–224.

Vazquez, Y. (2015). Constructing Crimmigration: Latino Subordination in a 'Post-Racial' World. *Ohio State Law Journal*, Vol. 76(3), 598–657.

Vieraitis, L. M., Piquero, N. L., Piquero, A. R., Tibbetts, S. G., and Blankenship, M. (2012). Do Women and Men Differ in Their Neutralizations of Corporate Crime? *Criminal Justice Review,* Vol. 37(4), 478–493.

Vigdor, J. L. (2013). Immigration and the Revival of American Cities: From Preserving Manufacturing Jobs to Strengthening the Housing Market. *Partnership for a New Economy and Americas Society/Council on Americas White Paper.* Retrieved from http://www.as-coa.org/sites/default/files/ImmigrationUSRevivalReport.pdf.

Warren, R. and Kerwin, D. (2017). The 2,000 Mile Wall in Search of a Purpose: Since 2007 Visa Overstays have Outnumbered Undocumented Border Crossers by a Half Million. *Journal on Migration and Human Security.* Vol. 5(1), 124–136.

Wasem, R. E. (2014). Noncitizen Eligibility for Federal Public Assistance: Policy Overview and Trends. Washington, DC: Congressional Research Service.

Wildemuth, B. (1993). Post-Positivist Research: Two Examples of Methodological Pluralism. *Library Quarterly*, Vol. 63, 450–468.

Willig, C. (2013). Grounded Theory in Methodology. In *Introducing Qualitative Research in Psychology* (3rd ed.), pp. 69–80. McGraw-Hill Education.

World Bank. (2011). Migration and Remittances Factbook 2011: Second Edition. Retrieved from http://siteresources.worldbank.org/INTLAC/Resources/Factbook2011-Ebook.pdf.

Appendix 1

Green Card Eligibility Categories (USCIS, 2020a).
You may be eligible to apply for each category if you are . . .

1. Green Card through Family
   - ❑ Immediate relative of a U.S. citizen
     - Spouse of a U.S. citizen
     - Unmarried child under the age of 21 of a U.S. citizen
     - Parent of a U.S. citizen who is at least 21 years old
   - ❑ Other relative of a U.S. citizen or relative of a lawful permanent resident under the family-based preference categories
     - Family member of a U.S. citizen, meaning you are the:
       - Unmarried son or daughter of a U.S. citizen and you are 21 years old or older
       - Married son or daughter of a U.S. citizen
       - Brother or sister of a U.S. citizen who is at least 21 years old
     - Family member of a lawful permanent resident, meaning you are the:
       - Spouse of a lawful permanent resident
       - Married child of any age of a lawful permanent resident
       - Unmarried son or daughter of a lawful permanent resident 21 years old or older
   - ❑ Fiancé(e) of a U.S. citizen or the fiancé(e)'s child
     - Person admitted to the United States as a fiancé(e) of a U.S. citizen (K-1 nonimmigrant)
     - Person admitted to the United States as the child of a fiancé(e) of a U.S. citizen (K-2 nonimmigrant)

- ❏ Widow(er) of a U.S. citizen
  - Widow or widower of a U.S. citizen and you were married to your U.S. citizen spouse at the time your spouse died
- ❏ VAWA self-petitioner—victim of battery or extreme cruelty
  - Abused spouse of a U.S. citizen or lawful permanent resident
  - Abused child (unmarried and under 21 years old) of a U.S. citizen or lawful permanent resident
  - Abused parent of a U.S. citizen
2. Green Card through Employment
   - ❏ Immigrant worker
     - Are a first preference immigrant worker, meaning you:
       - Have extraordinary ability in the sciences, arts, education, business, or athletics, or
       - Are an outstanding professor or researcher, or
       - Are a multinational manager or executive who meets certain criteria
     - Are a second preference immigrant worker, meaning you:
       - Are a member of a profession that requires an advanced degree, or
       - Have exceptional ability in the sciences, arts, or business, or
       - Are seeking a national interest waiver
     - Are a third preference immigrant worker, meaning you are:
       - A skilled worker (meaning your job requires a minimum of two years training) or
       - A professional (meaning your job requires at least a U.S. Bachelor's degree or a foreign equivalent and you are a member of the profession), or
       - An unskilled worker (meaning you will perform unskilled labor requiring less than two years training or experience)
     - Physician National Interest Waiver
       - Are a physician who agrees to work full-time in clinical practice in a designated underserved area for a set period of time and also meets other eligibility requirements
     - Immigrant investor
       - Have invested or are actively in the process of investing at least $1 million (or $500,000 in a targeted employment area) in a new commercial enterprise in the United States which will create full-time positions for at least 10 qualifying employees
3. Green Card as a Special Immigrant
   - ❏ Religious worker
     - Are a member of a religious denomination coming to the United States to work for a nonprofit religious organization

- ❑ Special Immigrant Juvenile
  - Are a child who has been abused, abandoned, or neglected by their parent and have SIJ status
- ❑ Afghanistan or Iraq national
  - Served as an Afghan or Iraqi translator for the U.S. government
  - Were employed by or for the U.S. government in Iraq on or after March 20, 2003, for at least one year
  - Were an Afghan employed by the International Security Assistance Force (ISAF)
- ❑ International broadcaster
  - Are coming to work in the United States as a member of the media
- ❑ Employee of an international organization or family member or NATO-6 employee or family member
  - Are a retired officer or employee of certain international organizations, or NATO, and certain family members
4. Green Card through Refugee or Asylee Status
  - ❑ Asylee
    - Were granted asylum status at least one year ago
  - ❑ Refugee
    - Were admitted as a refugee at least one year ago
5. Green Card for Human Trafficking and Crime Victims
  - ❑ Human trafficking victim
    - Currently have a T nonimmigrant visa
  - ❑ Crime victim
    - Currently have a U nonimmigrant visa
6. Green Card for Victims of Abuse
  - ❑ VAWA self-petitioner—victim of battery or extreme cruelty
    - The abused spouse of a U.S. citizen or lawful permanent resident
    - The abused child (unmarried and under 21 years old) of a U.S. citizen or lawful permanent resident
    - The abused parent of a U.S. citizen
  - ❑ Special Immigrant Juvenile
    - Are a child who has been abused, abandoned, or neglected by their parent and have SIJ status
  - ❑ An abused (victim of battery or extreme cruelty) spouse or child under the Cuban Adjustment Act
    - The abused spouse or child of a Cuban native or citizen
  - ❑ An abused (victim of battery or extreme cruelty) spouse or child under Haitian Refugee Immigrant Fairness Act (HRIFA)
    - The abused spouse or child of a lawful permanent resident who received his or her Green Card based on HRIFA

7. Green Card through Other Categories
   - Liberian Refugee Immigration Fairness (LRIF)
     - Are a Liberian national who has been continuously physically present in the United States since Nov. 20, 2014, or Are the spouse, child under age 21, or unmarried son or daughter over the age of 21 of a qualifying Liberian national.
   - Diversity Immigrant Visa Program
     - Were selected for a diversity visa in the Department of State's diversity visa lottery
   - Cuban Adjustment Act
     - Are a Cuban native or citizen, or
     - Are the spouse or child of a Cuban native or citizen
   - An abused (victim of battery or extreme cruelty) spouse or child under the Cuban Adjustment Act
     - Are the abused spouse or child of a Cuban native or citizen
   - Dependent status under the HRIFA
     - Are the spouse or child of a lawful permanent resident who received his or her Green Card based on the Haitian Refugee Immigration Fairness Act (HRIFA)
   - An abused (victim of battery or extreme cruelty) spouse or child under HRIFA
     - Are the abused spouse or child of a lawful permanent resident who received his or her Green Card based on HRIFA
   - Lautenberg parolee
     - Were paroled into the United States as a Lautenberg parolee
   - Indochinese Parole Adjustment Act of 2000
     - Are a native or citizen of Vietnam, Kampuchea (Cambodia), or Laos who was paroled into the United States on or before Oct. 1, 1997 from Vietnam under the Orderly Departure Program, a refugee camp in East Asia, or a displaced person camp administered by UNHCR in Thailand. American Indian born in Canada
   - American Indian born in Canada
     - Were born in Canada, possess at least 50 percent American Indian blood, and maintain your principal residence in the United States.
   - Person born in the United States to a foreign diplomat
     - Were born in the United States to a foreign diplomatic officer who was stationed in the United States when you were born.
   - Section 13 (diplomat)
     - Were stationed in the United States as a foreign diplomat or high ranking official and are unable to return home

Appendix 2

Full list of acts following definition from 18 U.S. Code § 1961:

(1) "racketeering activity" means (A) any act or threat involving murder, kidnapping, gambling, arson, robbery, bribery, extortion, dealing in obscene matter, or dealing in a controlled substance or listed chemical (as defined in section 102 of the Controlled Substances Act), which is chargeable under State law and punishable by imprisonment for more than one year; (B) any act which is indictable under any of the following provisions of title 18, U.S. Code: Section 201 (relating to bribery), section 224 (relating to sports bribery), sections 471, 472, and 473 (relating to counterfeiting), section 659 (relating to theft from interstate shipment) if the act indictable under section 659 is felonious, section 664 (relating to embezzlement from pension and welfare funds), sections 891–894 (relating to extortionate credit transactions), section 1028 (relating to fraud and related activity in connection with identification documents), section 1029 (relating to fraud and related activity in connection with access devices), section 1084 (relating to the transmission of gambling information), section 1341 (relating to mail fraud), section 1343 (relating to wire fraud), section 1344 (relating to financial institution fraud), section 1351 (relating to fraud in foreign labor contracting), section 1425 (relating to the procurement of citizenship or nationalization unlawfully), section 1426 (relating to the reproduction of naturalization or citizenship papers), section 1427 (relating to the sale of naturalization or citizenship papers), sections 1461–1465 (relating to obscene matter), section 1503 (relating to obstruction of justice), section 1510 (relating to obstruction of criminal investigations), section 1511 (relating to the obstruction of State or local law enforcement), section 1512 (relating to tampering with a witness, victim, or an informant), section 1513 (relating to retaliating against a witness, victim,

or an informant), section 1542 (relating to false statement in application and use of passport), section 1543 (relating to forgery or false use of passport), section 1544 (relating to misuse of passport), section 1546 (relating to fraud and misuse of visas, permits, and other documents), sections 1581–1592 (relating to peonage, slavery, and trafficking in persons), [1] sections 1831 and 1832 (relating to economic espionage and theft of trade secrets), section 1951 (relating to interference with commerce, robbery, or extortion), section 1952 (relating to racketeering), section 1953 (relating to interstate transportation of wagering paraphernalia), section 1954 (relating to unlawful welfare fund payments), section 1955 (relating to the prohibition of illegal gambling businesses), section 1956 (relating to the laundering of monetary instruments), section 1957 (relating to engaging in monetary transactions in property derived from specified unlawful activity), section 1958 (relating to use of interstate commerce facilities in the commission of murder-for-hire), section 1960 (relating to illegal money transmitters), sections 2251, 2251A, 2252, and 2260 (relating to sexual exploitation of children), sections 2312 and 2313 (relating to interstate transportation of stolen motor vehicles), sections 2314 and 2315 (relating to interstate transportation of stolen property), section 2318 (relating to trafficking in counterfeit labels for phonorecords, computer programs or computer program documentation or packaging and copies of motion pictures or other audiovisual works), section 2319 (relating to criminal infringement of a copyright), section 2319A (relating to unauthorized fixation of and trafficking in sound recordings and music videos of live musical performances), section 2320 (relating to trafficking in goods or services bearing counterfeit marks), section 2321 (relating to trafficking in certain motor vehicles or motor vehicle parts), sections 2341–2346 (relating to trafficking in contraband cigarettes), sections 2421–2424 (relating to white slave traffic), sections 175–178 (relating to biological weapons), sections 229–229F (relating to chemical weapons), section 831 (relating to nuclear materials); (C) any act which is indictable under title 29, U.S. Code, section 186 (dealing with restrictions on payments and loans to labor organizations) or section 501(c) (relating to embezzlement from union funds); (D) any offense involving fraud connected with a case under title 11 (except a case under section 157 of this title), fraud in the sale of securities, or the felonious manufacture, importation, receiving, concealment, buying, selling, or otherwise dealing in a controlled substance or listed chemical (as defined in section 102 of the Controlled Substances Act), punishable under any law of the United States; (E) any act which is indictable under the Currency and Foreign Transactions Reporting Act; (F) any act which is indictable under the Immigration and Nationality Act, section 274 (relating to bringing in and harboring certain aliens), section 277 (relating to aiding or assisting certain aliens to enter the United States), or section 278 (relating to importation of alien for immoral purpose) if the act indictable under such section of such Act was committed for the purpose of financial gain; or (G) any act that is indictable under any provision listed in section 2332b(g)(5)(B).

Index

About the Author

Malgorzata J. Zuber grew up in Kielce, in south-central Poland. She attended the University of Rzeszow in Poland where she earned an LLM degree in 2010 and a MEd in pedagogy in 2011. She moved to the United States in 2012 and enrolled in a criminal justice program at the University of Massachusetts Lowell. In 2014 she earned an MA degree in criminal justice, and in 2018 a PhD in criminal justice and criminology.

In the fall of 2016 she moved to Pennsylvania to continue her work at Alvernia University in Reading, PA. She is currently still working as an assistant professor at Alvernia University teaching mainly criminology, research methods in criminal justice, and current issues in criminal justice.

Her main research interests include immigration policy, intersection of immigration and criminal law, and criminological theory. Her articles have been published in Poland as well as in the United States.

www.ingramcontent.com/pod-product-compliance
Lightning Source LLC
Chambersburg PA
CBHW050613280326
41932CB00016B/3026